The Magpie Spoke to Me

How the Stories We Tell Shape Our World

BONNIE NADZAM

FOREWORD BY Jane Hirshfield

AFTERWORD BY Joan Halifax

SHAMBHALA

Shambhala Publications, Inc.
2129 13th Street
Boulder, Colorado 80302
www.shambhala.com

Excerpt from the forthcoming *Sarah in the In Between* by Neil Theise.
Reprinted by permission of Spiegel & Grau, www.spiegelandgrau.com.
Excerpt from *The Sound of Water: Haiku by Basho, Buson, Issa, and Other Poets*, translated by Sam Hamill, © 1995 by Sam Hamill. Reprinted by arrangement with Shambhala Publications, Inc., Boulder, CO. www.shambhala.com.
A short passage in this book was originally coauthored with Dale Jamieson and published in a different form in *The Carleton Voice*, Winter 2025 issue,
https://www.carleton.edu/voice/stories/the-case-for-spiritual-resilience/.
Reprinted with permission of Dale Jamieson.

Cover art: Sektor Creative Design/Shutterstock.com
Cover design: Kate E. White
Interior design: Anna Becker

9 8 7 6 5 4 3 2 1

First Edition
Printed in the United States of America

Shambhala Publications makes every effort to print on acid-free, recycled paper.
Shambhala Publications is distributed worldwide by Penguin Random House, Inc., and its subsidiaries.

LIBRARY OF CONGRESS CATALOGING-IN-PUBLICATION DATA
Names: Nadzam, Bonnie author | Hirshfield, Jane 1953– writer of foreword
Title: The magpie spoke to me: how the stories we tell shape our world / Bonnie Nadzam; foreword by Jane Hirshfield.
Description: First edition. | Boulder, Colorado: Shambhala Publications, Inc, [2026] | Includes bibliographical references.
Identifiers: LCCN 2026009528 | ISBN 9781645474753 trade paperback
Subjects: LCSH: Storytelling
Classification: LCC GR72.3 .N33 2026
LC record available at https://lccn.loc.gov/2026009528

The authorized representative in the EU for product safety and compliance is eucomply OÜ, Pärnu mnt 139b-14, 11317 Tallinn, Estonia, hello@eucompliancepartner.com.

"*The Magpie Spoke to Me*, a profoundly humane and quietly transformative read, is like water in the desert of an era dominated by the compulsive need to explain away mystery. In this beautiful book, Bonnie Nadzam offers something far more courageous and essential: reverent attention to the fullness of being alive. This book invites readers back into relationship with all that is: with grief, with the body, with the natural world, and with one another. Her stories are tender, unsettling, and deeply vital, inviting us to another way—a more aware way—of being in the world. Nadzam's capacity for storytelling is unparalleled—the prose is spacious, compassionate, and wise. This is a beautiful, important, and deeply timely book. I am better for having read it."—JOANNE CACCIATORE, PHD, best-selling author of *Bearing the Unbearable* and *Grieving Is Loving*

"A trove of wonders that made me glad to be alive and reminded me of all the unseen intelligences that have guided my own life. A catalog of mystery and the mystical that made me feel more in touch with the world."—MELISSA FEBOS, best-selling author of *Girlhood* and *The Dry Season*

"*The Magpie Spoke to Me* is a powerful reminder of the fundamental role of story in helping us shift from a 'cosmovision' of separation to one of wholeness that honors and respects the animacy of all beings. Through the stories she has collected and her potent reflections, Nadzam reveals how this story of wholeness is woven together by the numerous ways the spirit comes alive, in the mundane and the sublime, vulnerability and strength, the human and more-than-human. This book is a guide for participating in the story of our time."—EMMANUEL VAUGHAN-LEE, Sufi teacher, founder of *Emergence Magazine*, and author of *Remembering Earth: A Spiritual Ecology*

"Bonnie Nadzam has touched the pulse of life's essential mystery. She and I share Zen practice, but her book dances beyond Zen into the boundaryless. A coyote spoke to me in my twenties, and fifty years later, during a meditation retreat, a bluejay punctuated his remarks. Bonnie's book scatters such stories like starlight. What generosity! Don't miss her gifts."—PETER COYOTE, Zen teacher, author, and storyteller

"*The Magpie Spoke to Me* is one of those rare books that seamlessly weave together sophisticated theory with an intimate knowledge of the human soul to explicate a seemingly simple proposition: that our naturalized stories about the human are killing the Earth, and us. An accomplished Buddhist practitioner and writer, Nadzam's steadfast commitment to Life shines through the book's enthralling prose, showing

why, ultimately, at stake is nothing less than the re/construction of a relational ontology of the human as the foundation for novel ways of dwelling on the Earth."
—ARTURO ESCOBAR, author of *Pluriversal Politics: The Real and the Possible* and coauthor of *Relationality: An Emergent Politics of Life Beyond the Human*

"*The Magpie Spoke to Me* is a beautifully written book about storytelling—about how the narratives we tell ourselves and each other help us build and navigate our world. But, perhaps more profoundly, it's also about what we might call story*listening*, about how we can appreciate the richness, depth, and mystery of our relationships with the more-than-human world through an attitude of openness, receptivity, and wonder. Bonnie Nadzam combines scholarly research, philosophical reflection, and spiritual insight to engage with essential questions about the role we play within the cosmos, whoever 'we' might be."—MATTHEW LIEBMAN, the Justice for Animals Endowed Chair and Professor of Law at the University of San Francisco School of Law

"Reading this book feels like sitting at a ring of stones around a small fire, listening to the deepest truths of the human spirit. Nadzam's beautiful offering honors the uncapturable knowledges that modern life so often crowds out. It is a generous, life-affirming gift to anyone seeking a more relational way of being."—BERNIE RHIE, Zen Teacher and Associate Professor of English at Williams College

"How do we tell—and how do we listen to—stories that do not fit our inherited maps of reality? The stories in this collection, together with Nadzam's reflections, challenge dominant assumptions and frameworks that often constrain our thinking. They invite us to enlarge our sense of what is possible, to bear witness to a world that is more porous, stranger, and more intimate than our current maps allow."
—WILLIAM EDELGLASS, Director of Studies at the Barre Center for Buddhist Studies

"Bonnie Nadzam and her many storytelling companions tell of happenings that seem dramatic and uncanny to the critical, scientific mind. A writer and Zen adept schooled in other kinds of mind, Nadzam wants us to understand that the normative view we have of the world we live in, and the world we see coming, is a view, one among many, and, like all views, is both true and false. If we want to see a bigger future, with bigger possibilities, she implies, maybe we better think twice about what we take to be real."—NORMAN FISCHER, poet and Zen priest, author of *When You Greet Me I Bow* and *Selected Poems: 1980–2013*

FOR DALE JAMIESON

Whose intellectual brilliance I have always trusted
the more for his profoundly loving spirit

Let us not begin with definitions. With academic references.
With proof that many books have been studied on the subject.
With the notion that for an idea to be singular, purposeful,
or even useful it must be backed up by the research of others.
Let us begin with a smaller gesture.

—CHRIS ABANI, "Ethics and Narrative"

Can we bear to look at what we have not told ourselves? Can we hear what we do not know?

—JOAN HALIFAX, *Being with Dying*

Contents

Foreword

STORIES ARE HOW KNOWLEDGE—navigable, unnavigable, and useful for navigating—slips inside us, then stays. They are also how knowledge is made malleable: Stories are multiple and multiplying, a turning kaleidoscope of possible views and versions. They shape and reshape our relationships to what is around us and to our history. Then, too, stories are spiderwebs. They catch knowledges otherwise uncapturable, knowledges outside other modes of seeing or telling. This book reminds us that it is the complex and uncapturable knowledges, still somehow conveyed, that change how we feel about our lives, and that change, as a consequence, how we may lead them—not as separate and isolated selves but as parts of larger wholes, conversations, and communities.

A basket woven sufficiently tight and made of just the right grasses can hold water, carry it, lift it to mouth, let us drink. A story can be like that as well: one way that always-passing, always-changing experience is made holdable by, brought inside, the life that goes on—taken into its blood vessels, muscles, emotions, thoughts, decisions. For this, our human heart-minds and spirits have turned always to stories. Have turned, sometimes, into stories, ones that we ourselves then tell to help ourselves, and all of us, remember who we are.

In the time before the invention of writing, the only way to keep information in place was to set it into some form so memorable that it could be repeated without the entropy that makes the children's game telephone both humbling and funny. In telephone, a sentence whispered from one person into the ear of another in a not-that-large circle comes out at the end as an entirely different sentence. But if you add memorability's woven grasses, words travel without losing shape and shedding precision. For me, the best way to feel this is to have someone ask me how many days there are in May or November. To retrieve the answer, my mind starts at once to silently recite the mnemonic learned in childhood: "Thirty days hath September, / April, June, and November . . ." That we repeat this rhyme still using its now archaic "hath" shows how powerfully binding the glue of memorable repetition remains over time.

In the time before writing, memorability meant, most often, two strategies of thought's embodiment. One is the music of poetry's meters and rhymes. The other is the memory-engraving arc of a vivid story: The experiences that transform understanding and transmute one relationship with reality into another want to live on in our lives. From these modes of preservation came Homer's epics, Korean myths, the dream songs of Australia, the griot songs of Africa, the instructions in wisdom held in the Indian Vedas, the stories filling this book; came the early science of Lucretius's *De Rerum Natura,* Shakespeare's plays, and the Chinese novel *Monkey.* Came every culture's storehouse of stories that tell of exemplary human lives and, equally, of the fates, comic or tragic, of our human delusions. These stories hold sometimes facts (the names and geographies of the islands Odysseus stopped at, returning from Troy), sometimes the inventions of imagination (the faculty that lets a person, the sum of persons, and a culture explore, speculate, dream, and, through its limitless instrument, perhaps see more).

Fairy tales hold hopes and also warnings of things not to do. Parables put into our human minds and lives the wisdom of animal ways and natural history—what a fox knows is different from what is known by a turtle. The myth of Arachne combines the pondering of spiderwebs and human weaving, without necessarily sorting which may have come first, and adds to it a warning against human pride. Koans propel a person from one condition of being and understanding into another. Ghost stories tell us there are things to be known beyond our usual knowing. Sufi teachings let us laugh at ourselves in ways both memorable and instructive.

In myths and fairy tales, ghost stories and Sufi teaching tales, human, animal, and inanimate realms and beings are not kept separate or apart from one another. In a story, any part of observed phenomena can become a teacher. This unboundaried taking-in is true also in a life. We learn from trees. We learn from housecats. We learn from floods, earthquakes, wildfires.

The non-separating perceptions of metaphor and myth hold humanity's aboriginal recognition of our broader kinship and continuity with other forms of existence. In languages worldwide, words for what is felt to be "good" speak of increase, rising, growth; decrease and descent are signals of peril or death. These are knowledges taken from plants and animals, from seasons, from the rising and setting of sun and moon, and their associations feel foundational and go mostly unquestioned. But then the storehouse-stories come, bringing nuance and complication. In some stories, darkness can become a house of richness and mystery, a place of safety. Not-knowing might be recognized not as failure but as a needed antidote to hubris. The stories of riddles teach what they individually hold but also a larger message: that sometimes a person needs to think in ways beyond linear logic, to think by feeling, by leap, by empathy's emptying us of all concept of self and other.

In stories and their taking-in, we learn to say yes to the actual, often difficult, often bewildering life any human being must live. We learn, too, that we are not alone: Someone else has left a breadcrumb trail through the roadless woods. Religious parable, Zen koan, manga, joke, science fiction or speculative-future novel . . . stories shape us and bind us together. But we must not idealize. Some stories work also to keep us apart. It's important to remember that stories are a neutral technology: They carry whatever they're given.

We have never needed better ones than we do now. This book invites its readers into their finding and their saying.

—JANE HIRSHFIELD, 2025

The Magpie Spoke to Me

Introduction

All of this is about permission.

—PÁDRAIG Ó TUAMA, *In the Shelter*

I had rescued a very sick young rat whom I named Tailer and needed to find him a companion as rats don't do well alone. I got in touch with a rescue organization and drove to New Jersey, right over the George Washington Bridge. I brought home an older female rat who hated me and particularly hated Tailer. After a week, I realized I needed to bring this angry, mean rat back to the rescue. So I drove back to New Jersey, and just as I was crossing the bridge, she started getting agitated, as if she wanted to get out of her little travel cage. I reluctantly opened the cage door and then she climbed up my arm, sat on my shoulder next to my ear, and said thank you. When we got back to the rescue, she flew back into her pile of friends in their big enclosure.

—Lori Gruen, philosopher and ethicist, Chicago, IL

When I was about five or six, I levitated in my living room. I was alone and standing facing the couch, and I scooped the air by my sides with my hands and launched myself above the floor just a couple of inches. It was an effort similar to lifting off the floor of a pool while standing in a shallow end, and it felt good and it was good. I will never forget that feeling.

—Cameron Mesirow, musician, Boston, MA

I'm picking peyote in the desert in Texas near the border and come across a rattlesnake with a head the size of my hand, just coiled up on this big brain of peyote that I want to pick because people need them for prayers. So there I am, talking to this giant rattlesnake. "Would you please move," I say, "because right under you there's some prayers I need to collect." And the snake moves. "Hey," I say, "thank you." I pick the peyote, and I put some tobacco down, and the snake winds right up around that peyote again.

—Henry Oso Quintero, founder of RedInk Institute, Santa Cruz, CA

I have a memory that is real, that is clear and intact, and that I know is not mine.

—M. H. Tse, animal law scholar and director of the Museum of Human Predation, Hong Kong

I woke up with my sister, who had died three years earlier, right at my third-eye center. I was looking through her like a pair of glasses.

—Carrie Garman, licensed professional counselor, Cleveland, OH

FIRST THINGS FIRST: This is a book about storytelling, but it is not a book on craft. And though I consider myself an artist of sorts, and I am the author of many works of fiction, it is not a book about the arts or aesthetics. Further, while I am an ordained Zen Buddhist priest and a serious student of Zen, this is not a book about Buddhism or any single religion.

Importantly, however, many questions regarding human experience that arise in the stories collected here have long arisen for me in Zen practice—even before I knew it was "Zen" I was doing. So a few words about the practice may be useful here and there. As a little preliminary context, Zen is a meditation practice that is secular insofar as it is of this sensory world, engages the physical body and critical thinking as primary tools, and does not appeal to the sacred, transcendent, or supernatural (even if it doesn't deny them); it is spiritual insofar as it is deeply experiential, appreciates intuition, and interrogates being (if not meaning). I live my life and proceed in this book with the understanding that the spiritual and secular tell a single story in two voices and that it is not always easy to tell which voice is which. This does not trouble me.

Further, I am certainly no scientist; this book is definitely not about science. Nor am I attempting with this book to frame, interpret, or hold up scientific studies or observations of any kind, though I do quote actual scientists—some I know personally, some I don't—in many places. And though this book is in part a gathering of others' stories—their experiences of and relationships to various phenomena—I am no ethnologist or anthropologist, though I do quote some of them, too. Rather, I have gathered stories for this book from human beings I consider kindred spirits, as it were—"my people." (There is a lot to say about the importance and challenges of finding in a lifetime one's people.) There is no controlled study here. It's taken me a lifetime of experiences to arrive at a place where I had just this collection of phone numbers and email addresses, and just this inclination to ask just these people, and where those who contributed had just the right amount of time in their schedules to generously share. Some of them are colleagues, some family, some old friends, some fellow poets and writers. For each contributor, I have included a name, occupation, and place of birth. There are many countries and continents represented in these stories (all more or less by accident). Some contributors were patients or clients I met in various personal, clinical, or hospital settings in my capacity as a chaplain, and those names and details have been withheld and changed to protect them. I offered every contributor the option of sharing anonymously, and some of them took it.

My prompt for these contributors—and for you, reader—was this: Have you ever had an experience you feel you have to precede with something like, "I know this sounds crazy, but . . ."? Experiences that, however apparently small or insignificant, shifted your understanding of the world and your place in it, or indeed, dissolved a little of your understanding of these things? Was it an experience that you yourself resisted? And have you kept it to yourself, perhaps because you appreciate that our "reports of" or stories about these experiences might be pathologized or dismissed as fantasy? These are experiences that suggest something about the sense of reality you have adopted from your culture and contemporaries, or ancestors, might be . . . incomplete. Modern habits of credibility may exclude whole categories of experience before they can be described. Where do you go within yourself to check in to see if something is true or right? And if you don't have such a place, how do you discern?

I begin this introduction with disclaimers, of a kind, because I am of course cognizant of the increasing extent to which, in the United States, anyway, so many people seem profoundly distrustful of experts and expertise. I am not. I tend to defer to experts and expertise with gratitude and respect. Though in places in this book it may strike readers that I am disavowing technology or modern science or rational thinking, I am not. Technology, modern science, and rational thinking provide us exquisite tools (Western medicine, for example, and feminism, and many of the innovative, life-affirming applications of global and US law I study in my day job); as a solidly middle-class American, for better or worse, I live a life of ease and comfort because of many of these tools. However, we should no more use a fork or a hammer for every task than we should use technology or modern science or rational thinking on every occasion. And the occasion at hand is sharing the experiences we've had that have jolted us *out* of our regular way of being and thinking—linear thinking, dualistic thinking, and yes, rational thinking. Experiences we've had when it felt like the gap between subject and object—just for a moment—closed. I was swallowed by a mountain. The tree gave me the answer. My grandmother was a bird. The stars are my cousins. I changed the weather. I dreamed of all this before it happened. I dreamed all of this as it was happening. The leaves were moving all by themselves. I could feel the physical pain and terror of the cows in the truck on the highway. The mountains told me to go home. The magpie spoke to me.

This *is*, then, a book about a birthright we all share: experiencing being human, which includes not so much *making* meaning of our experiences and existence but rather, as grief counselor Dr. Joanne Cacciatore puts it, allowing meaning to emerge. And one of the most important and ancient ways that meaning emerges among humans is through storytelling—not just stories in books or in any kind of publication but stories told out loud, over dinner, around a fire, at funerals, on walks, in the boardroom or staff room, in the dark, at parties, alone to ourselves or to an intimate partner on the soft, frayed edges of sleep. Stories that are lived, told, relived, reshared, and from which, alongside thousands of other such stories, whispers and hunches regarding our shared purpose on Earth may indeed begin to take shape.

For short, you might say this birthright I'm referring to is one of fundamental creativity, but I worry the words *creative* and *creativity* have by now been a little shorn of their true meanings in relation to the production and consumption of media, including stories of all kinds. By creativity I do not mean artistic production: I mean the ordinary human power to shape a shared world through attention, language, silence, and response. Reports of our human experiences may be dismissed or diminished by others because they don't jibe with the tools of rational, linear thought, for example. But we ourselves may also dismiss and diminish them, because so many of us have grown distant from our storytelling roots, attributing instead that role, where it is considered important or significant, to professional creative writers or filmmakers who do or aim to make a living thereby and whose stories are commodified in the process. We empower these creative types to be teachers—to a great extent, the only teachers—of how stories can or should be told, and we measure the success of such stories as we measure many things in the Western world—that is, by the amount of money, status, or reputation they generate. From where I stand, this all seems such a distortion of the storytelling impulse.

Last year, I was invited with a small group of artists to spend a week at Plum Village, a Buddhist monastery of the Plum Village tradition in the Dordogne, southern France, near the city of Bordeaux. It was founded by two Vietnamese monastics, Thích Nhất Hạnh and Chân Không, in 1982. We were not asked to make art while there, and most of us very much did not want to; unasked to do so, musicians had left their instruments at home. Writers were not writing, filmmakers were not filming (though there was much spontaneous song). At one point, we were called upon by the monks to cocreate something as artists—and we collectively sort of pushed back. That was not what we had come to do (ultimately the leaders among us choreographed something very beautiful). What many of us were curious about and looking for instead was how—in a world that asked us to be literally productive with our artistic skills and inclinations—to find the original ground from which those intuitions and compulsions to create art had originally arisen in our lives. I'm sure nobody did this in a week, and that many, if not most, artists hold related questions in their heart-minds all the time.

It is not first and foremost a product we make with our stories; it is not a career or a life situation we most fundamentally make by way of storytelling; it is a world we are making—a single, shared life. A story is not only a report of what happened. It is an act that alters relation. What is told, withheld, or deformed enters the conditions under which others live. If you think you are not a storyteller, please, think again. If you think your stories do not matter, how I hope this book will change your mind. Every story shared, distorted, or withheld participates in the world we are making together. Ours is a world that is always—even amid destruction and darkness—in a state of potential and becoming. My hope would be that you tell *every* story to *some* being, even "just" to some otherwise quiet night or open field, and that you leave nothing out.

My role has been to carefully gather these accounts and make a hospitable space for them. It has been, metaphorically speaking, that of a person sitting at a ring of stones around a small fire sawing and snapping the dark as I listen to some of the wildest, most deeply personal stories of those gathered around me. Every personal story offered—to anyone, anywhere—is sacred. By *sacred*, at its best, I mean every story shared changes the terms according to which we can listen—if we're really listening. So perhaps reverence for that, too, has been required of me, and I humbly ask it of each of you as you read. In many instances, sharing these stories and putting their names beside them has taken courage. Some folks I asked knew they had such experiences but couldn't remember them. Some declined my invitation to contribute because they had never had such experiences, or because they were afraid to share them. Two friends and colleagues expressed concern about sharing their experiences and including their names alongside them. What would people think? I find it very interesting, even amazing, that any of us should be so afraid to share a human experience; it is a fear I both understand and share. Otherwise I would not have taken on this project.

In the pages ahead, though I reflect on various global cosmovisions (for the time being, you can consider this like a worldview) within which some of these experiences are considered acceptable, some not, neither I nor any of the contributors really attempt to explain *why* any of these experiences occur, nor what they *mean*. We are just talking around the fire, trusting that eventually, slowly, sometimes with wonder and joy and sometimes with sharp awareness of great suffering, meaning—or at the very least clarity regarding appropriate and loving action—will emerge. "We are all one lesson,"[1] Alice Walker says. And we are always still learning it.

This book makes a simple claim: Stories do not merely describe the world; they create the world we inhabit together. I did not know what stories would come to me over the last year, but as I slowly collected them, I began to see how they were lining up of their own accord—as drops, then gathering pools of water, eventually creating shallows, then channels that braided themselves into a stream with life and purpose of its own. And what I noticed was that this stream, as it were, ran parallel with many of the motivating, sometimes academic, sometimes deeply personal questions and rites of passage I have experienced—from prayer in Catholic grade school to my first period of zazen with a sangha, to startling one-on-one lunches with my first Zen teacher, to a dissertation about literature of the long eighteenth century, to priest ordination, into motherhood, chaplaincy, and up to this morning's sitting and assemblage of school lunches. I have accordingly, and gently, I hope, arranged the stories offered to me with framing commentary that reflects this alignment.

My hope is that this book opens more room in ordinary life for difficult, disorienting, or unwelcome stories to be told and heard. My hope is that this book, if and once read, is set aside with encouragement, if not confidence, in opening a little more space for storytelling in your own life—in the kitchen, around the fire, at funerals, in bed—especially for telling and listening attentively to those stories that are challenging, if not wholly unwelcome, in some of our larger circles.

As such, this is not a book for the world, for the country, or for the classroom. It is for *you*. It is not an attempt to redefine how stories should be told or how the universe should be described—what counts, what doesn't, who's right, who's wrong.

Take this book, if you would, draw a small circle in the dirt before you, then step inside of it. What's it like being you *right there*? Each of us can only begin with our own life—the only place where any of these questions can be experienced and tested.

"Feel your feet on the ground," Joan Halifax writes. This is where your life is happening.

But allow me to begin again properly, if I may, with a story.

–1–

Ghosts?

The universe shows us only the shadow of its mystery.

—FREEMAN DYSON, *Disturbing the Universe*

Every morning, my mother, a widow at the time, would feed the birds that came to her patio. She especially loved the ruby-throated hummingbirds. Hours after her death, I sat at my desk, heartbroken, grieving, holding a lock of her hair. My desk faced a large window with a view of the garden. Suddenly, a ruby-throated hummingbird flew close to the window, nearly touching the glass. It hung there, suspended, looking at me, for a long time. The next morning, I sat at the breakfast table in my garden, once again overwhelmed by sorrow. A second hummingbird, perhaps the same one as yesterday, appeared in front of my face, impossibly close. It hovered, outside all ordinary time, looking right at me. Helen. Mother.

—Melissa Pritchard, novelist, San Mateo, CA

When I told Zoyla, the servant at the farm, that I had to leave with the armed men, she immediately burst into tears. Seeing her reaction, I, who had been strong until that moment, completely broke down, and my first tears erupted uncontrollably, as if someone had opened a tap. My voice was completely choked. I had to breathe deeply and ask for strength from within, and I suddenly realized it wasn't the adult me who was crying; it was my scared inner child, Pascualito, who felt the fear. The adult does not feel fear—only the child does. So I addressed that child inside me: *I love you. I love you. Relax, nothing is going to happen. I am here to protect you.* That internal resolve was how I managed to overcome that first emotional crisis [as I was being kidnapped], stepping back into the role of the experienced, vigorous adult I needed to be to face the journey ahead.

I was ordered to dismount after a long ride, and when the *compas* took the saddle off my horse, I realized I had lost the animal as well as my freedom. They released the horse right there, and I overheard the commander angrily ask why they had done so, as "the field was mined." The injustice I felt was overwhelming, forcing me to cry out inwardly: *Holy Virgin, intercede for another miracle. Save that horse. Let it not step on a mine. For the field was mined.* It was an act of profound cruelty toward a creature that had done nothing wrong but only served and served.

While immobilized in that restricted area of the camp, sitting on a log, I began to realize how completely cut off I was. I reflected on my profound lack of knowledge regarding the language of the flora and fauna, recognizing it as an enormous oversight and a waste. I desperately felt the need to communicate with the nature surrounding me, seeking to capture its energy or find something that would comfort my spirit. I knew that nature had its own language and sounds, but I needed a special message appropriate for the moment I was living through. This silent longing was answered when a hummingbird suddenly stopped right in front of me, accompanied by a strong ray of light. I immediately understood this to be the most divine message from God, assuring me that my loved ones were with me and that I was not abandoned.

—Pascual Contreras Flores, educator and farmer, Bochalema, Colombia

I spent a couple of months writing and shaping a song called "Deep Forest" about being responsive to the call of life.

So I booked a week of studio time with a friend of mine, Drew, who is a wonderful producer down in Somerset—knowing that while I love the creative process (the act of writing and making music), I have always found the recording part painful, even in the best of conditions.

It was an intense week, and on the penultimate day of recording, just as we were editing the final part of the song, I could hear unusual birdsong outside the studio. It's a modern building beside a house, set among fields and trees, and the sound was getting louder. I mentioned the sound to Drew, and as we turned, suddenly this beautiful pair of swallows flew into the studio, circling above our heads, calling. I stood, then quickly sat back down again, as we watched them fly a few loops before leaving the way they'd come in.

The curious thing wasn't just that they'd flown in (which in Drew's many years of working in the studio had never happened before) but that they'd flown in just as we were working on the final part of the song, where the refrain is "Will you call on me . . . I am one with the void from which life comes."

—Nathalie Nahai, author, artist, speaker, and musician, London, England

ONCE, DECADES AGO, at the Zen Center of Los Angeles (ZCLA) on Great Dragon Mountain, situated since 1967 on Normandie Avenue in Koreatown, my fellow Zen practitioners and I were gathered in the big empty room of the Dharma Hall for a *teisho*. A teisho is a formal talk given by a Zen teacher that, translated from Japanese, means something like "presentation of the shout." It is like a lecture, except the subject is often the unknowable, and the professor is a Zen master, or near to. I suppose a teisho might also be analogous to a sermon—but curiously, I feel this analogy is somehow less on point. I hope this book might clarify some of the difference in function among such kinds of talks, and those who present them, and why.

The "shout" on this particular day was being presented by Roshi Egyoku Nakao, now my primary Zen teacher and then abbot of the temple. Somewhere in her remarks that afternoon, she referred to the Gate of Sweet Nectar service. This is a ceremony that incorporates practices from the Vajrayana tradition, Japanese Shingon, and Tibetan Buddhist rituals, for those to whom such matters are of interest (and please, do bear with me—this is really not a book about Buddhism or religion). At ZCLA, the Gate of Sweet Nectar service is offered on Sundays, and the numinous chant that we sing was written and set to music by Krishna Das—a creation prompted per request by Bernie Glassman, the renowned teacher of American Zen and the founder of the Zen Peacemakers (worth a lookup!). A quick internet search will turn up YouTube videos of the service, as well as Krishna Das offering the sung prayer. It is profoundly beautiful.

The Gate of Sweet Nectar is a powerful ceremony whereby participants aim to gather all the "hungry ghosts"—all of them, throughout all space and time—together into our midst and then feed them. A good rough-and-ready definition of a hungry ghost might be any being tormented by desire—by insatiable hunger and thirst—and who you can draw on your own (I recommend giving it a try) with a teeny-tiny mouth; an impassably long, skinny throat; and an enormous, unfillable stomach. In this ceremony, we extend an invitation and the spiritual food (alongside actual food pantry donations) to every hungry ghost among us—including the living and the dead, all those suffering from injustice, and to those parts of our individual selves, too, that are "lost and left behind." We are addressing and beckoning all within us that is neglected, forgotten, abandoned, oppressed, abused, or otherwise "in shadow," as the Jungians (and many Zen practitioners) would put it. In short, no one and nothing is excluded from the invitation.

But the Buddha Hall at ZCLA, even the beautifully spacious zendo at Great Plains Zen Center, in the Driftless, where I long practiced with Roshi Susan Myoyu Andersen—these are spaces you can measure in square footage; there isn't room for every being throughout all space and time. So, for some, the intention of this ceremony is or must seem symbolic or metaphorical. For others, I suppose, it does not register as even that meaningful. But for the rest of us, everyone is invited and everyone comes. There is no good area or volume problem to represent how this works out mathematically, though there might be an application in some emerging fields of physics.

In the ceremony, we sing together:

Calling out to hungry hearts
Everywhere through endless time
You who wander, you who thirst
I offer you this Bodhi mind
Calling all you hungry spirits
Everywhere through endless time
Calling out to hungry hearts
All the lost and left behind
Gather round and share this meal
Your joy and sorrow
I make mine.

When in this service I am in the role of *ino*, or "chanter," who sings the first round of these lyrics alone, my voice always breaks in the same place—on the fifth line; it is so literally unspeakably moving, I can hardly utter the words. I add this just to offer some measure of how deeply experienced the ceremony can be. And I say this having been raised Catholic—having memorized the Mass, as is the custom—and as someone who spent her adolescence (middle school and high school) in fundamentalist, evangelical Wheaton, Illinois. I have never been a stranger to ceremony, ritual, or prayer. But this Gate of Sweet Nectar ceremony was the first one I performed with not only my entire heart and mind but also every atom of my body, as the practice trains us to do. I was doing, for the first time, what in the afterword of this book, Roshi Joan Halifax encourages all of us to do:

> Step fully into and trust your lived experience. Entrust yourself to your own attention, to your breath. Where are your feet, right now? What is the light like around you? What are you hearing? It takes deep and abiding attention to be fully human.
>
> Why hold back? Yes, we can turn away from our lived experiences and the ways they challenge our relationship to each other and the world. We have that choice, and we have devised ingenious and myriad ways to turn away from them. But we can also turn toward our experiences.

In Zen practice, your body is your only map—ignore it to the detriment of your practice and profound diminishment of your life. Likewise, in the practices encouraged in this book, the body is not an obstacle to truth but its site. The body is not to be mortified, ignored, mistrusted, whipped into obedience, or otherwise denied. For example, the meal ceremony in which we eat together is in my lineage called *oryoki,* which means "just enough." Everything "your body" shares with "you" is useful if not extremely important information. Every emotion—which arises first physically and then, on a good day, can be identified and considered and named in words, however "unwelcome" the feeling might be—is an opportunity and a tool. One can step into lived experience, of course, in the midst of anything; it need not be already considered but can thereby become ceremony. What does body awareness, body intelligence, have to do with engaging fully and completely with what it is to be human? Why *do* we hold back from it, when we do? How exactly, in Halifax's words, does stepping into our lived experience challenge our relationship to each other and the world?

In Egyoku Roshi's teisho on the day in question, she spoke at least once of these aforementioned hungry ghosts who, she noted, *do* in fact gather around in response to our invitation and call.

At that, a longtime resident of the temple, for whom I had and have much respect, raised her hand and responded to our abbot and teacher with something like, "Come on. I appreciate what you're saying, but the ghosts actually come? Like, they show up? It diminishes our practice to talk this way. When can we get real and stop talking this way?"

(Maybe such questions have already registered with you, too, reader. [So soon?] You're not too sure whether or how to trust this book, or where this is all going.)

Ghosts, this person at ZCLA was suggesting, of *course* didn't *actually* gather around in the Gate of Sweet Nectar ceremony—what kind of talk was that? Zen is respected in many circles for jibing so *well* with some aspects of Western science; isn't it basically secular? And isn't it true that neither science nor Zen relies upon scripture or belief? Don't they share an empirical approach to observing reality? (If you're curious, a quick internet search of "Buddhism" and "Western science" will generate scores of relatively reliable—that is, peer-reviewed—papers and sites that detail correlations between Buddhism and quantum physics, for example, including some ways in which the apparent paradoxes of the former may help us grasp what seems just so incomprehensible and impossible about the latter. Such an internet search will also, of course, generate scores of *un*reliable papers and sites.)

So ghosts? Showing up when beckoned in a ceremony rooted in ancient Eastern traditions but taking place in Los Angeles in 2007? Can we get real, please? It was a totally good and fair question. And Egyoku Roshi was both serious and pleasant when she responded: "That is your experience. I am speaking from my experience, in which the hungry ghosts show up."

In emphasizing her own experience, Egyoku Roshi, like any Zen teacher, was not attempting to undermine anyone else's experience. She was not replacing evidence with anecdote, or reason with imagination, or experience with expert knowledge; she was not trying to shortcut the assigned reading for the class, which she had skipped to stay up making TikTok videos; nor was she attempting to shut down conversation or to validate her identity as a Zen teacher over a student's relative ignorance. Rather, she was encouraging each of us to engage in the practice we had presumably come to a Zen center to learn: to look deeply into our own nature. There are many Zen koans (situations, stories, or dialogues presented by the teacher that must be lived rather than studied) that demonstrate this fact: Any teacher worth their salt does very little teaching and a lot of facilitating to ensure students' independent experience and, where appropriate, drawn conclusions.

"A teacher is someone who points the way," Bodhidharma said, "but you must see it for yourself." Huangbo, a Tang-dynasty Zen master, puts it like this: "The foolish seek the truth outside themselves, not knowing that it is within." And Walt Whitman: "You shall no longer take things at second or third hand . . . nor look through the eyes of the dead . . . but look with the eyes of the living."[1] (Was there ever a more beautiful imperative to set a book on a shelf while also carrying it somewhere in your heart-mind as you step outside to live and *experience* it?) I remember amid Zen training taking my qualifying exams at the University of Southern California, where I argued (with no small amount of personal bias at that point in my life) that the worst and possibly most unethical books in the world were books on the craft of creative writing. (I have not read any of these in a couple of decades, so I don't know what the best of the newest might entail. I do have a short stack of these here at home, for a rainy day.) Though he was (of course) writing about genius, I argued, even Immanuel Kant says it is the "innate mental aptitude" of the student through which "nature gives the rule to art."[2] T. C. Boyle was on my advisory committee, and at the table—now *there* is an excellent teacher—and he said to the other faculty, "She's right. Very little teaching goes on in a creative writing classroom." May it always be so.

But back to the Buddha Hall and the teisho and ghosts. I was relatively new to the practice at that time—I was all in, I thought, but I was new. And this exchange gave me real pause. I have never forgotten it. At the time, I was working on that aforementioned PhD in English, and so, somewhat paradoxically, I was being trained to value and emphasize rational analysis in pretty much all exploration of fiction and poetry. (Theory was always and ever supposed to be as rigorous as the sciences; however much it actually ever was, or is, that's another good conversation for another day.) In fact, it was partly because of my appreciation for and focus upon incisive analysis, deductive thinking, philosophy of language, and logic that I trusted the practice of Zen, which encourages questioning, skepticism, critical thinking, and the same kind of curiosity I'd always brought to academic study. Importantly, too, I trusted (and still trust) Egyoku Roshi—not despite the fact that she is a human teacher who refuses to act the mystical guru but because of it. And if she said the ghosts showed up—well, I did not know what to think. *Is* that what she was saying? Ghosts as in—*ghosts*?

This certainly did not jibe at all with my experience of apparent reality. Clearly, I resolved, I would have to sit zazen more, and experience apparent reality more, and with greater attention. After all, if you wanted to sum up Zen practice in five words, you could do no better, I think, than to say, "Sit down. See for yourself."

I can see myself and my fellow practitioners gathered in that room, most of us cross-legged on the floor, most of us shifting uncomfortably this way and that in our pointy, awkward bodies, most of us with deeply furrowed brows as we tried very hard not to think in discursive loops about what was being said. It is a rich and wonderful memory that seems like a long time ago, and I love each and all of those individuals so much. If I made for you now a little list of the fleeting observations I've made over subsequent seasons about this apparent reality I was determined to experience more or better, a "list of ghosts," as it were, that I myself have by now seen, well then perhaps you, too, would raise an eyebrow and set this book aside, wondering, *Can we get real, please?* Or maybe you'd read on, giving me the benefit of the doubt, but with certain academic categories in mind to accompany you, just in case: ecofeminism, say. Without something like that to support your rational skepticism, if you did happen to read further, you might categorize this book in a certain, perhaps dismissive way, in order to make sense of and distance yourself from it. It may be titillating, or entertaining, but it certainly couldn't be serious or worth taking seriously. For others among us, the question is simple, though not easy to live with, as the unraveling of both the biosphere and relative geopolitical stability of the last half century are reason enough to go, okay, so obviously we're missing something. Obviously something about the way we conceive of existence is . . . off. Perhaps for those of us who fit in this category, it is *precisely* rational skepticism that we are engaging. In *Conjectures and Refutations,* Karl Popper writes, "The rational attitude does not consist in the possession of knowledge, but in the readiness to admit that one may be mistaken."[3]

What changed for me over that and subsequent seasons was not that I came to know what ghosts are but that I stopped confusing disbelief with discernment. So, banal and disappointing as it may seem, what such a "list of ghosts" in my life so far has amounted to would not be a series of supernatural phenomena I now know all about but that years ago I was too square to realize. (Please also note that psychedelics and/or drugs and chemical substances of any kind are not the subject of this book; in my view, what you are most likely to learn from being on drugs is what it's like being on drugs, just as what you are most likely to learn from eating pancakes is what it's like eating pancakes.) Rather, it would be a list of things I thought I knew—things I'd taken for granted but am no longer certain about. I would put on the list things: Time is linear and moves in one direction; "reality" is a thing that can be seen; consciousness arises from the human brain; dreams are "less real" than life awake; the rational mind is the best and most, if not only, sane tool for navigating a life. A more critical tool, it now seems to me, is not only my capacity for reason but the information and experience of my entire body. "My great religion," writes D. H. Lawrence, "is a belief in the blood, the flesh, as being wiser than the intellect. We can go wrong in our minds. But what our blood feels and believes and says, is always true. The intellect is only a bit and a bridle. What do I care about knowledge. All I want is to answer to my blood, direct, without fribbling intervention of mind, or moral, or what not."[4]

I was in the middle of work in a restaurant kitchen when I suddenly realized I was upside down in space, then there was no top or bottom or sides to anything, even as the floor was pressing up against my feet. And somehow this all meant nothing I was worried about mattered at all. This single experience completely changed my sense of the world, even though it only lasted a split second. Early on I worried that the positive effect would wear off, like a hit of something. But it never has.

—Anonymous, Dallas, TX

I was in the final round of a competitive job interview for a position I really needed and thought I wanted. We were seated at an oval-shaped table—me and four other individuals who were questioning me—when I was suddenly pierced with understanding I could never explain. I felt it straight through my face. I did not want this job. This job would be the end of me. I stood up and politely and maybe awkwardly said I had changed my mind about the position. They remained friendly and smiling, I think because they were all so shocked or confused. I apologized and excused myself from the room. When I recall this, I feel wonderstruck, even relief, but no regret, especially since I have a good job in the same field now. I'm not sure what I was picking up on, but it was something. I haven't run into any of those individuals workwise, but I'm not sure it was one of them anyway. It was just something about the recipe of that moment and the weird knowledge it delivered, weirdly, to my face.

—Anonymous, Northfield, MN

True story: I knew I was a girl since age six. Yet I learned early on that it was not socially acceptable for me to be myself if I wanted to avoid shaming and ridicule, so I pretended to be tough and just one of the guys. Circa 2010, I was on active duty in the Coast Guard at Fort Wadsworth on Staten Island, New York. As part of one of those intramural sports team-building events during a spring basketball tournament, I was attempting to show my shipmates that I could play basketball. I mean, after all, I was on our middle-school basketball team that won our regional championship. Good enough to make the team but not a starter, so I rode the pine the entire season and only got to play if our team was winning by a lot of points. However, I can forever say I was on a winning basketball team to claim status as a baller.

Nevertheless, I played basketball before, but my shipmates had never seen me play until the tournament. I had on all the basketball gear there was to wear . . . armbands, loose-fitting shorts, a tank top jersey over a T-shirt, and a pair of sneakers. I looked the part. Even in warm-ups, I looked good. The game started. Our team had the lead near the end of the first half, so Coach put me in the game. I got my hands on the ball and was quickly fouled; therefore, I had two free throws coming my way. Oh, how I despised free throws because all eyes were on me. So, I'm at the line. I bounced the ball three times, raised the ball over my head with both hands before I took my first shot. I hit nothing but the backboard, not even close to the rim or the net, and I could hear my shipmates gasp like, "WTF, I thought Petty Officer Magnetek was a baller." My second shot hit the backboard, this time inside of the square, then bounced inside the ring. One point scored. I think . . . I don't know. I was too busy calming the mortification inside of me to notice. I kept playing until the half ended.

In the second half, our team switched sides of the court. I got back in the game much earlier this time. I made a great defensive play and stole the ball. My shipmates cheered. So here I am, dribbling down the court, open to take a shot, but I didn't jump and shoot like I learned to do in middle school, so the dude defending me blocked my shot with one hand, all ball to the point I was stuffed and couldn't jump even if I wanted to, so I came down awkwardly. My shipmates had had enough of me, so the coach pulled me out of the game. I sat on the bench for a while, watching the real ballers play until one of them got tired. Coach told me to go back in, but for some reason, I couldn't move off the bench. I couldn't get up because the muscles in my back had tightened up. This was new to me and my body at thirty-three years old. I told my shipmates I couldn't move, so Coach called Coast Guard medical, who arrived with a stretcher. If missing the entire goal and having my shot blocked wasn't embarrassing enough, I had to be rolled out on a stretcher in front of everyone, who all applauded in knowing I was safe and had not suffered a serious injury. I gave them a thumbs-up while being rolled away on the stretcher to the medical office.

Turns out it was only a back spasm, which could be easily cured with a little rest, muscle relaxers, and a couple of standard military cure-all pills—ibuprofen—to remedy. At home, lying down with an ice pack on my back and my toddler crawling all over me, I thought to myself that I had no business out there playing basketball, knowing damn well I really can't play basketball and was just faking the funk (something my dad says about the pitfalls of pretending and not being truthful), attempting to prove myself as masculine when I was not. Being something other than myself did not fare well with me that day. I should've listened to my parents. Albeit this behavior carried on for two more years before I came out of the closet as a transgender woman and began to live my life truthfully.

—MoHagani Magnetek, writer and anthropologist, Fairbanks, AK

–2–

Ontological Malaise

Those who do not have power over the story that dominates their lives, power to retell it, to rethink it, deconstruct it, joke about it, and change it as times change, truly are powerless.

—SALMAN RUSHDIE, *Imaginary Homelands*

Never lose a holy curiosity.

—ALBERT EINSTEIN, "Letter to William Miller"

My first remembered visit from someone who had died was when I was twenty-five. I had always been afraid of nighttime visits from vampires, axe murderers, werewolves, bogeymen, and even small aliens that might be waiting to drop from the ceiling or crawl up from the floor. I was "afraid of my own shadow," as my father said. Literally terrified of the dark. Nonetheless, I hadn't ever thought to fear ghosts. When one finally showed up, it wasn't even in the dark but broad daylight. I wasn't even particularly surprised, except perhaps for where and when it happened. In a synagogue on the Jewish Day of Atonement, Yom Kippur, 1984, our family pet dog Misty came to visit me at the time of her death.

I was staying with two friends in a borrowed apartment in the downtown Manhattan neighborhood called SoHo. We attended a small Orthodox congregation nearby. The three of us abstained from food or drink from before sunset at the holiday's start until after sunset the next night. We were diligent with the other observances. We wore no leather goods, for how can one ask forgiveness of God for one's sins while standing in the skin of another being? We stayed in synagogue until late the first night and were among the first to arrive early the next morning. Staying in synagogue without substantive break all the way through to the ceremonial closing of Heaven's Gates after dark, we hoped all our penitential prayers would be answered.

I was on my feet for the long late-morning standing prayers. These were followed by the alternating boisterous and yearning melodies that accompanied the taking of the Torah scrolls from the ark. In the middle of song, I suddenly had a strong sense of being watched, from my right side. As I turned, a middle-aged woman with shoulder-length, dark brown hair, in synagogue-appropriate conservative dark dress—long-sleeved, skirt below the knees, high collar—entered my field of view. She was standing by the wall beneath a window, gazing at me, with a smile warm, patient, and affectionate. Yet as my head completed the turn, she wasn't there.

Next thought: *How could I have seen a woman standing on the far side of the men's section?* (In modern Orthodox synagogues, men and women are seated separately, often to either side of the hall. There could have been no woman standing there.)

Next action: I glanced at the clock on the wall. Five minutes past noon.

Next thought: Misty is dead.

No idea where that came from.

The whole little incident was over in a quick moment and felt more confusing than creepy. I shrugged it away.

After seven more hours of ritual atonement and a fasting headache, we returned to the apartment. As per dutiful habit, I immediately called my parents to see how their fast day had gone. My father answered the phone crying. It's the only time I can recall him crying.

He handed the phone to my mother, and she explained to me that they had to put Misty to sleep. Our pup had sort of disappeared after her morning walk. At first they assumed that she was, as usual, napping in the sun on my brother's old bed, but when she didn't show up at the sound of the refrigerator opening, they went looking for her. She was found curled up, hard to rouse, under a couch. There was blood coming from her behind. They brought her straight to the vet, and he told them she probably had colorectal cancer and advised putting her to sleep. Comfortable in my father's arms, she had received the injection, fell gently to sleep, and was quickly and easily gone.

"What time?" I asked her.

A few minutes after twelve.

—Neil Theise, from his memoir Sarah in the In Between, *forthcoming from Spiegel & Grau*

I HAD FOUND ZEN PRACTICE in Los Angeles in my mid-twenties and amid a painful and disorienting (and ongoing) path of trying to become a mature adult. I wanted to find the place of the wise. My first Zen teacher was John Daishin Buksbazen, a professional psychotherapist in his seventies, just this wonderfully rich, colorful, cranky, absolutely and radically nonjudgmental and honest old soul—with a lot of years of zazen and a lot of perspective on the practice, its institutions, and being human. It was over hot sake in a crowded sushi bar that I relayed to Daishin something of the anxiety around trying to become a published writer, why I thought I wanted to, and so on, and he gave me some unusual advice in response: "Don't tell stories." He subsequently explained to me that a student should never let their teacher's sake cup go empty.

"Would you like some water, too?" I asked him, having refilled his little sake cup.

"No," he growled. "Water isn't good for leather."

Don't tell stories. How could that be anything but discouraging advice for a would-be writer? And indeed, how can such a phrase be at all integral to a book about the importance of storytelling? It's a phrase I first learned in grade school; it meant *don't lie.* It's not that Daishin thought I was lying about anything, and his suggestion wasn't meant to address my professional or artistic self-doubt and frustration alone. What he was cautioning me against was delusion on a much bigger scale. It was the kind of delusion that treats mental constructions as truth; that reframes mysteries as solvable puzzles; that proposes endless solutions where there are no problems; and that in the twenty-first century offers people so many slick ways of defining, identifying, and branding a self that the often provoking, sometimes seriously unsettling questions of *Who am I?* and *What is going on here?* may never trouble you at all. Among the most disturbing developments in this vein may be the extent to which we have come to understand ourselves as and are understood to be consumers. For many powerful individuals, global corporations, and institutions, the data that comprise our consumer profiles is the most important and only valuable identity we have—a concept of selfhood and a sense of worth we tend to reinforce effortlessly.

It was the simplest, most natural thing in the world for me to bypass all questions of who or what I was, why earth, why stars, why fingernails and hair and birds in the so-called sky—to skip over the breathtaking mystery of it all—so that I could get down to the business of *becoming a writer.* (I'm overstating it a little, though it sure was easy to grow anxious about how and when to merge into the celebrity literary culture while a writing student—perhaps especially in LA.) And I thought it was the most natural thing in the world to more or less disregard our lunch and the restaurant as "background" against which to engage questions about the difficulty of *becoming a writer.* I sensed but did not accept what I accept more fully now: There is no such thing as a background. Ever. Anywhere.

After life in LA, writing became one expression of this question for me, but the question itself was larger than literature. The matter of stories and storytelling Daishin was opening up in conversation had little (though not nothing) to do with writing fiction and would have pressed upon me amid any career I might have pursued. What he was nudging me toward and what I eventually came to appreciate is that repeating any narrative or system of beliefs about the nature of my life was almost always an attempt to relieve the kind of anxiety that was roused by precisely the aforementioned questions: *Who am I?* and *What is going on here?* The stories he cautioned me to stop telling myself were the conceptual explanations that pretended to answer such questions. The temporary, unsatisfying answers might range from the very personalized and highly specific "I am a PhD candidate at the University of Southern California" to the highly general but no less abstract and even speculative "I am a human." If this last statement strikes you as inarguable, consider what my friend, the international peace speaker and founder of First Voices Radio, Tiokasin Ghosthorse, once told me and that we discussed more fulsomely just recently: There is no word for "human" in Lakota.

So while in my California grad-school classes I was examining text, with Daishin I was being encouraged to examine life itself—and since life, death, too. And not just any life but my life. My actual minute-by-minute life. Have you ever made your object of study your completely physical, embodied, minute-by-minute life? Not thinking or reflecting upon it but diving into your sensual experience of it? The sound, smell, touch, taste, sight of it? And then, when escaping safely into the realm of reflection, diving back into sensual experience again? A few summers ago, on an island off the coast of New Hampshire, I led a group of interfaith adults, many of them elderly, in fifteen minutes of zazen. Afterward, a septuagenarian and his wife approached me, astonished, having realized that it was very likely the case that neither of them, in all their days, had ever before sat still experiencing their own bodies for fifteen minutes. Isn't that something? They asked for some "tips" on trying this again on their own. There is a common suggestion for helping guide Zen practice to feel every pore of your skin; that is a great exercise. Or I love the one where you imagine for a moment that you are a deer being hunted in the woods, and you have 360-degree awareness (if a twig were to snap a quarter mile behind or before you, you would hear it); then drop the fear and the sense of being hunted and maintain that physical, 360-degree awareness.

"Know that you are the object of your own seeking," says the eleventh-century Islamic philosopher and mystic Al-Ghazali. Where are your feet right now? Examine yourself, Paul says to the Corinthians. Test yourselves. Sit in your cell, and your cell will teach you everything.

In LA, writer, fellow student, and dear friend Bryan Hurt and I used to employ our new theory chops to refer to this aforementioned anxiety as our persistent "ontological malaise" (something like despair about the state of existing). If cold beer at Venice Beach didn't help, we certainly gave it a good try. However my answers to these anxiety-making questions might shift, I always had one, even when I was unaware of the question, which was most of the time. Another way to navigate the answer to these anxiety-fueled questions, Daishin was suggesting, was not to answer at all. Recognize each answer for what it is—a concept, maybe even a really good one, a *genius* one—and just allow the questions to simmer. When anxiety wants assuaging and existential dread needs a "story" to tuck it in, there is another inclination within—one that is neither sourced in nor addressing the anxiety or the dread—and it wants to get curious. Daishin implored me—in so many moods and in so many tones of voice, from the gentle and wonderstruck to the irritated and exhausted—to *get curious.* In a silent retreat of even just a couple days, there is, for better or worse, nearly endless opportunity to ask oneself, *Who am I? Who?* hundreds, thousands, hundreds of thousands of times. "Ask it with your *whole body*," he said, in line with Joan Halifax's words about entering fully into our lived experience.

Consider the opposite way of being, which I still practice unthinkingly more often than I wish were the case: first deciding who I am and what's going on, and then, like, acting it all out. This can look like defining myself based on ideas I have, mostly preferences and aversions, with little receptivity to the nuance of what's arising around me. From this ground, it seems important to have a firm opinion, to be consistent, to be highly individualized; all action and speech must correspond to the idea of what I say I am. So if I'm an artist, then I'd better spend the day making art. When I'm on such ground, which has a paradoxical tendency to fuel the flames of anxiety, I'm not appreciating what being creative means—that stripped of its fantasies, each of our lives is essentially creative; that responding to a friend in need may be the ultimate creative act called for by the day, even if a poem or a sketch goes unfinished; that it is this life and this world that we're making, one action at a time. Minute by minute. Second by second.

Indeed, this is integral to a central premise of this book: that we create reality with the stories we tell, so we had better at least be aware of what those stories are and among those stories, which of them we are prohibited from sharing or are afraid or hesitant to share. Because what we leave out—what we refuse to say, are afraid to say, or are incapable of saying because we have not entered fully into our lived experiences—all of this too shapes our world profoundly.

A few clarifying words, I hope, regarding the meaning(s) of the word *story* in this book (for now, I'll leave fiction out of it):

- A person has an experience and shares a report of this experience with another. This is a story. (This is at, if not itself, the very heart of being human.)
- A person has an experience and is hesitant to share any report of it, so they do not. This is an untold story. (There are many

reasons, even some good ones, that a person may not want to share an experience with another; this book focuses on stories we don't tell because we fear we will discredit ourselves by sharing them, as they don't jibe with mainstream cultural values and ways of being.)

- A person has an experience and either loves or cherishes the experience so much (for any number of reasons) that they try to repeat it or somehow capture and perpetuate it; or a person has an experience and analyzes it, discovers its meaning, and either lives by or attempts to impart upon others its meaning and importance: This is "telling stories." It is certainly not *always* "delusion," as this kind of "telling stories" has many critical functions (think Western science, where its applications are life-affirming), but this is also what Daishin, as an elder and as a teacher of Zen, cautioned me against when investigating the nature of my life.

In the pages ahead, I'll unpack each of these lines a little further; I think it helps to distinguish among them.

–3–

Cosmovisions

It was at night on a long, dull drive from Northfield to Fargo. It was very dark, just prairie and darkness, a couple months after my dad's death. I was listening to public radio, some interview with someone, when all of a sudden I smelled my dad strongly, kind of a mix of sweaters and books but distinctly my dad's smell. I turned off the radio and looked around for him, held out my hand, asked if he had something to tell me. I then heard him in my head saying, "Turn on the radio and scan to the next station."

I was in the middle of nowhere and had no idea of the local radio stations. The scan stopped and a song started to play, "Father and Daughter" by Paul Simon. I'd never heard it before. The chorus was "As long as one and one is two, there'll never be a father who loves his daughter more than I love you."

I pulled off the highway sobbing, no light in sight. It was so visceral, it was so completely nonconceptual and intimate an experience with my father that I said to myself, *Shame on me if in the years ahead I ever question this experience or others' experiences like it.* I will never doubt the reality of my experience.

—Peggy Hanson, certified Jungian analyst, Moorhead, MN

When I was thirty-nine, I knew enough not to reproduce again. I had dreamed of my first child before his birth and knew him immediately when he arrived—our long-imagined kid, finally here, plucked from my dream and living into his blond, curly-headed self. Our days were a string of bright lumps of clay, each one mashed and molded to form the new shapes our family would take. It was barely possible. My husband had begun to show the first signs of the chronic fatigue that would come to shape the rest of our days. And yet I had imagined her all my life, my second child. She'd be the fourth cornerstone of my dream house, the other kid filling the back seat where I gazed, wondering who would arrive to sit there. She'd use up space, plastic spoons, Band-Aids, bottles, break her million things. She'd be carried on a plane to see the place her mother grew like a weed on the arid prairie. *Who needs another white kid?* I asked myself, knowing the sins my ancestors left to fester. And yet one day I passed a smoke bush taller than a house and knew, despite expense, despite wreck, exhaustion, scarcity, despite all evidence: I believed that plant was kin to me, her lacy russet blooms effulgent in the late spring light, reaching higher than any smoke bush I'd ever seen, sending her pollen out despite the shift in winter. I had to do that, too. When he arrived (since there would be no she), I knew he made no sense, like me, a stray seedling with its problem root. And yet, "You sing me song?" he asks, his red hair gleaming like the world's most glorious sunset.

—Mary Austin Speaker, creative director at Milkweed Editions, Dallas, TX

SAYING THAT WE CREATE REALITY with the stories we tell sounds a little abstract, even whimsical. Maybe even as "out there" as a world of hungry ghosts, talking rats, and a smoke bush as kin. Let's take a step back and start by broadening our shared understanding of what a story is. In fact, a shared understanding is itself a useful way to define it. For our purposes, let's add to this rough-and-ready definition that a story explains phenomena and experience using language and symbols. So, "Noah was six hundred years old when the floodwaters came on the earth" is a story. So is "Little Red tucked her basket under her arm and headed into the dark wood." So are "$4Fe+3O_2 \rightarrow 2Fe_2O_3$" and "Organisms with heritable traits that increase their chances of survival and reproduction are more likely to pass those traits on to the next generation." So is "Last week an atmospheric river dumped several feet of snow on the Sierras in California." So are these: "I am writing these pages in 2025"; "I am over here, and you are over there."

How a person reports a personal experience, or tells a story, is almost always rooted in their cosmovision. It's worth pausing to consider what a cosmovision is and means, as it differs meaningfully from a mere "worldview." A worldview is like an opinion—however deeply informed or uninformed it may be; a cosmovision, however, is something you inhabit—sometimes unconsciously. For example, a very reasonable worldview about the weather might be that a sudden summer storm is caused by atmospheric pressure, temperature gradients, and wind patterns; an understanding about the weather from the cosmovision you inhabit might be that a sudden summer storm poses risks and is an inconvenience, but it is not a message, a relative, or an ancestor. Alternatively, you may indeed experience a sudden summer storm to be a message, a relative, or an ancestor.

A couple more examples of a cosmovision: You don't merely believe (as with a worldview) that bodies of water are important resources; rather, you live your life as if they are. What else could they be? Alternatively, if you inhabited a different kind of cosmovision, you wouldn't merely believe that bodies of water were alive; you would live your life as if they were. How could you treat or be in relationship with them otherwise? Hopefully by these few very attenuated examples, you can begin to appreciate how powerful a given cosmovision (whatever it is) can be.

A person tells a story or shares an experience that is *rooted* in their cosmovision when they don't explain their world as if to an outsider, but when they tell it from within their lived reality, where many shared understandings are assumed. For example, if I say, "I really like being in nature, and just last weekend I hiked out into the San Juan Mountains for a little peace and spiritual reflection," then enjoying being in nature, what it means to hike out into it, and that peace and spiritual reflection can be found there . . . all seem to merit little or no explanation. But if you were to share these same words with someone living in a different way, place, or time, where this shared reality of modern Western life is unfamiliar, your weekend mountain report would need much explaining. "There's nature, which is mostly the world out of doors, and there's the human world, a lot of which happens inside," you might begin. "Nature includes places such as mountains and forests and preserves, maybe backyards and parks, and the human world includes cities and towns and buildings. . . . You can be in nature, or out of nature, and you can drive into nature, you can hike into nature, you can bike into nature . . . and out of it again . . . whenever you wish." And on and on you would talk, perhaps bewildered and even for the first time confused by having to explain "what everybody knows" and what you had taken to be a given.

Scholars in narrative anthropology say that stories, especially folklore and myths, embody the assumptions of a culture's vision of reality. They describe storytelling as a process of cultural transmission, sensemaking, and identity formation. In these ways, storytelling *reveals and reinforces fundamental conceptions of human existence and the cosmos.* In other words, stories are cosmovisions made visible.[1] To this, I would like to emphasize the importance of examining what we call folklore and myth and what about our own modern lives we consider to be above or beyond or more real than folklore and myth (to say nothing, for now, of the stories that we straight-up pathologize). *Every* cosmovision influences *what stories are told in this way,* and those stories in turn shape how people *internalize* that worldview.

Including this one: "I really like being in nature, and just last weekend I hiked out into the San Juan Mountains for a little peace and spiritual reflection."

This example I've shared—the weekend mountain report—is an example of the eurowestern cosmovision, which most of us can be particularly blind to seeing as cosmovision, rather than simply "reality," precisely because we inhabit it. According to this eurowestern cosmovision, humans are separate from nature—which goes a long way toward explaining the weekend outing in the mountains. For better or worse, our shared world has become one in which most people at least know about and appreciate the currency of the eurowestern cosmovision. For those in our contemporary world who *don't* inhabit *only* this eurowestern cosmovision, however, who have their feet in two worlds, as it were, there tends to be more awareness of moving in and out of different ways of being, as circumstances require. For example, a caregiver, a migrant worker, an immigrant or a refugee, a speaker of multiple languages . . . would likely have rich perspectives on navigating multiple cosmovisions as a matter of survival. (There are many terms for this in various academic fields, including double consciousness, code-switching, cultural brokering, and more.)

Last year, I was at a conference talking with a professor of philosophy about this tendency among Westerners to be blind to our cosmovision as cosmovision, and he responded with three points that, whether designed to achieve it or not, effectively shut me up. First, he told me, there is only one reality and it can be empirically observed and measured. Second, nothing about this is open to rational debate. And third, he said that he hated it when people invoke "Western" as in "Westerners" as opposed to anybody else. We stood there with our name tags, held captive by reason. There was no meaningful conversation or connection available.

If you're with me even a little bit, though, on how it is that the stories we share from our lives are almost always rooted in our cosmovision, whether we are aware of it or not, then let's consider a little further how it is that the stories we tell create the world we live in (or the world we live *with*, depending on your cosmovision). It is aphoristic and commonplace to say that storytelling creates and transmits culture—but creates the world itself?

Imagine two women standing on a city street in Denver, Colorado. The first of these women, woman A, experiences herself as an individual looking out on the city, observing other people, the state capitol, pigeons and crows, trees and garbage, and the distant crooked line of the Rocky Mountains. She stands as if at an Archimedean point, a hypothetical viewpoint from which she has an objective perspective, which serves her as a starting point for reasoning or taking action. She is independent and autonomous; from her vantage point, much of the world can be explained, measured, and described via rational resources and means. She can subtract herself from the street and the city she is observing in order to comprehend it. She is here, in her body, perceiving, assessing, and judging reality with increasing accuracy per the tools of her culture, and reality is "out there." Hers is the eurowestern cosmovision.

It is generally from this ground that most of us tell, receive, read, and write stories of all sorts—both the kinds of reports from our life we'd share with friends and loved ones, as well as the kind some people write down and publish (and including most, if not all, fiction). Some of us may think we already see the flaws in this kind of view. At this point in the twenty-first century, we may already have good evidence that it has an all-too-obvious dark side. But it is important to acknowledge that it took centuries of revolution—political, cultural, socioeconomic, scientific—for woman A to arrive here. Her apparent autonomy and the tools she uses to describe her world rationally have proven powerfully liberatory for many humans.[2] Hers is also likely the conventional way of being for most people, most of the time—and this is remarkable. And, really, seriously questioning the universality of this woman's way of being—standing here, assessing reality out there—is very difficult for most of us, even if some of us like to say words such as *interdependence, interconnected,* and *oneness.* To question the fundamental, universal truth of her sense of the world around her might be to unravel one's entire understanding of self, the cosmos, the real, and the possible.

For the other woman on the street, woman B, there is no Archimedean point from which she can view the city, its buildings, people, river, or animals as "out there." She cannot view the city as if from aside anything at all. There is no aside, and there is no backdrop. She cannot subtract herself or the act of her observation from anything she is seeing and must take this into account when considering what kinds of actions to take in the world. For her, nothing exists extrinsically or independently; everything is mutually constituted, so much so that there is no subject or object, no independent "self" looking out at a "city." Indeed, woman B does not experience herself as the center of anything, neither the street nor the scene around her. If asked, she might state that the state capitol, pigeons and crows, other people, trees, garbage, Rocky Mountains, and even distant planets all have the same fundamental ontological value (though each with its own function), like so many parts of a single body. Her cosmovision is a relational one, and it may seem quite radical. That's because it is. She is experiencing being human the way my friend and colleague, the Chilean scholar Macarena Montes Franceschini, describes it here in an experience she had in Germany.

There's a feeling I can't name, one I only experienced during a brief stage of my life. I've tried so hard to feel it again, but I never have. It was the end of March 2021, and I had moved to Germany with my two dogs rescued in Chile: Uva, a mixed breed with a big personality that people often mistook for a German shepherd puppy, though she was really an adult with short legs; and Mora, a calm and kind black Lab with an enormous appetite. My husband drove us from Barcelona so I could begin my PhD research stay at the Max Planck Institute. Because the dogs were too big to travel in the plane cabin, he drove us the entire way.

I rented a small ground-floor studio with a private yard in Dossenheim, a quiet town next to Heidelberg, so Uva and Mora could have outdoor space. The neighborhood was surrounded by open countryside. I rode my bike to the office through fields, sometimes in rain or snow, sometimes past rows of lettuce, strawberries, and flowers. Every morning, afternoon, and evening during those four and a half months, I walked with Uva and Mora through the fields that stretched around us, with forested hills rising behind. Just Uva, Mora, the other creatures living in those fields, grass, shrubs, trees, mud, hills, and me—all witnesses of that space and time.

This feeling would come over me completely, as if it filled my whole body. It was as though the boundaries of my body melted into Uva and Mora and the land around us. It gave me goose bumps, brought tears to my eyes, and filled me with a warm light. I felt a profound appreciation for the present moment. Everything was okay. Everything was in order. I felt supported and part of something, even though I was alone in a new country without my husband, family, or friends.

Part of that feeling was gratitude for being in the fields with Uva, Mora, and nature, but it was more than gratitude. I keep a daily meditation and gratitude practice, writing down what I'm thankful for each day. I admit that sometimes I do it in pursuit of that feeling, trying to summon it back, even to force it back, such an embarrassingly human thing to do. But it never returns. I fear it may have been a once-in-a-lifetime experience. I fear I may never feel it again.

I've been to breathtaking places since, such as the Amazon, the Colombian Caribbean, and Santiago after the rain when the Andes are covered in snow. I've achieved great things, such as completing my PhD, working and studying at Harvard Law School, walking along the Charles River, and driving through the fall foliage in Vermont. I have a wonderful husband, family, and friends whom I love deeply. But I still haven't felt it again. It seems this feeling has nothing to do with achievement, travel, or even human connection.

Perhaps that feeling was what true interconnection between humans, nonhumans, and nature feels like: just Uva, Mora, the trees, the fields, the wildflowers, the mud, the bugs, the hills, and me. No expectations, no worries, no social conventions, no need to say *Guten Morgen* to passersby, no ambition, no taking, no accumulation, no faking, and no need for more.

Uva and Mora have since passed away, leaving an indescribable emptiness, and with them, perhaps, the capacity to feel that feeling again. As a human, I get caught up in *my* projects, *my* work, *my* worries, *my* problems, and forget that I belong to a *We*. I forget to look around me. I forget my mother's advice not to stare at my own belly button. But forgetting doesn't mean it's lost.

That connection still hums quietly beneath everything I do. Uva and Mora embodied that interconnection with the whole and its parts. I was simply fortunate to experience, for a brief moment in my life, the marvelous simplicity and complexity of dissolving into them and into everything.

—*Macarena Montes Franceschini, animal rights and rights of nature scholar, Santiago, Chile*

HOW WISE SHE IS, MACARENA. She knows that, as Annie Dillard puts it, "the pearl cannot be sought . . . although it comes to those who wait for it, it is always, even to the most practiced and adept, a gift and a total surprise."[3] While that may be so, here are some wise words attributed to Shunryu Suzuki: "Enlightenment is an accident, but practice makes you accident-prone." I respect and aspire to Macarena's stance nonetheless; for hers are surely the words of one who is poor in spirit and who appreciates the importance of letting go of the experience totally if there is to be any hope of ever again experiencing her life so fully and completely (without the residue of her wonderful memory).

I remember early on in Zen practice, Daishin joking to me about how much Zen monks cherish their memories. At the time, I didn't get it—how easy it is to get hung up on wanting to repeat some peak experience. But if you sit on your meditation cushion thinking you know what you're looking for, or worse, hoping to find again what you once found, "you are mountains and rivers away from it"—or so Zen practitioners are guided by the remarkable "Sandokai" poem.[4] In his essay "The Possible and the Real," the French philosopher Henri Bergson explains the same phenomenon when he compares our meager and insufficient mental abstractions and gymnastics (however brilliantly modeled they may be) to the unrepresentable "continual creation of unpredictable novelty that seems to go on in the universe" with every passing moment and that is as fresh, new, incalculable, and unforeseeable in our inner lives as it is in the so-called outer world.[5]

In the imagined Denver street corner scenarios above, again, woman B experiences the world relationally; no one and nothing exists independently. Woman A inhabits the cosmovision I myself adopted without even being aware of adopting anything at all, born as I was white and solidly middle class in Cleveland, Ohio, to a nurse and a welder, later raised in a Chicago suburb chosen for the good public schools. Mine was the mainstream Western culture's cosmovision that describes a single, objective reality that science, politics, and economics should and can manage and explain. All the buildings of all the strip malls, and all of the early iterations of McMansions and the many, many churches in suburban Chicago, they seemed pretty fixed and steady; the Canada geese kept to their side of the park and never talked to us, the tree canopies bonneted the safe streets in a pretty and decorative way, and time was a thing that progressed steadily forward, carrying each of us on our own separate journeys to college. (Don't get me wrong—I had a pretty wonderful, even unusually wonderful experience as an adolescent in that sheltered, privileged, and well-resourced town, and I remain grateful for every bit of it.)

I never questioned the cosmovision outright because I was not aware of it, and I was not aware of it because I was not particularly suffering. I was in most ways on the benefiting side of this cosmovision that, after all, has indeed given rise to many wonderful people, things, ideas, art, drugs, technologies, and innovations.

But I *did* have this kind of ache. Do you know this ache? What Rumi called something pulling on the soul—a kind of longing that was always meeting what I was told and mostly believed were the hard edges of things. I oriented myself toward people and activities that seemed to fuel the ache because somehow I knew it was trustworthy and needed to be tended like a flame or cultivated like a garden. There was this call of things—from the horizon line where the remaining prairie met the sky to the teaspoon on the kitchen table to the very particular orange of the red-breasted robin. There were individuals, too—teachers who stood out. James Langlas, our English teacher, comes to mind, who stood so quietly before us, smiling, waiting for us to settle into stillness, and whose heart, it seemed, had somehow in his decades of teaching high school English enlarged to divine proportion. You could tell that it had just by his posture as he stood there waiting. It would seem he was teaching a book, holding a paperback copy of *The Mayor of Casterbridge* as he moved around the room, but he was also silently announcing—did anyone else see it?—that the lesson at hand was something else, something beneath the book, behind the hand, and sometimes he'd catch my eye and I knew that he knew I knew. It *was* something in his posture; it was the light in his eyes; it was the way he stepped from the front of the room to the chalkboard and how he'd lift the chalk. He wasn't overtly spiritual or spooky or serious; he was animated, alive, engaged, ready. He was a small man who seemed in all ways, including literally, light on his feet. I can picture him bracing the air with his empty hands as if he were holding a ball of light—a gesture he often made to emphasize a point. When he wasn't teaching English, Dr. Langlas was a tae kwon do teacher, and in fact, an eighth-degree black belt, a grandmaster who served on the US Taekwondo team and in 1974 won a gold medal in the International Taekwon-do Federation World Championship in Montreal. His body awareness was profound, and there was nothing accidental in the way he moved.

But I did not know how to answer into the moment of any of this or what kind of responsibility it entailed. And I would forget what I'd seen, or I'd doubt it. I knew it and I didn't know it. I knew it and I didn't quite accept it. I knew that once I accepted it completely, I would have to live my life in accordance with it, whatever it was, or at least try wholeheartedly to do so. As a matter of fact, years later in LA, I passed Daishin's meeting house every day for nearly a full year before I went in. I knew once I did, my life would change forever. Just this morning I was listening to a recorded talk by Wendy Egyoku Nakao, and she said, "Once you turn over a rock, you have to turn over *all* the rocks." She held a beat of silence, then, and from the audience before her in the room, in that quiet pause came the faraway sound of a single man laughing.

It was a single phrase that struck me—enough that I pulled to the side of the road and typed it into my phone. Why that? Why then? I don't know. The world is always trying to tell me something. This was from my reading. I had remembered a character, an investigator, standing at the scene of the crime, asking himself, *What am I not seeing here?* I didn't try to puzzle it out just then. With unexpected gifts, I don't ask. Such gifts are proof against rational pressure—they yield best if left alone.

What am I not seeing here? It was only later that I thought of Poe, his "Purloined Letter." Another investigator, the celebrated Dupin, is searching high and low for a document. He has looked in every possible cranny. Nothing. Finally he asks himself, "What's the least likely place someone would hide the thing?" The answer comes right away. It would be hidden in plain sight. These detectives, the best of them, are metaphysicians.

Then, later in the day I remembered Henry James's novella *The Beast in the Jungle*. The protagonist, Archer, has lived his whole life convinced that he will be granted some great revelation. He passes his days, his years, poised in expectation, his attention attuned elsewhere. It's only when it's too late that he realizes that there will be no such event and that, in the waiting, he missed the thing he had been given. I offer a crude summary of a subtle story and I apologize.

When the philosopher Pascal died, it's said that his servant found a folded note sewn into his waistcoat. It was a written record of a profound spiritual experience that he wanted to keep always near, lest he forget.

I understand that. We have our great insights and then we move on. I don't know how many times I've marked a moment—Always remember this!—only to then forget. These revelations shine in their occasion; it seems then they might solve everything. But the occasion is displaced by all the other occasions.

What am I not seeing here? The question is, I see, a bookmark, a reminder taking me back to something I seem to have known forever, which I can't keep in the forefront of my mind. It's embarrassing. Because it's the awareness of the gift itself—the thing that all the actions of living so effectively obscure. I don't need to put it into words. It can't really be put into words. There's the saying: Don't sweat the small stuff, and it's all small stuff. Whoever came up with that? *Nota bene*: It's not.

—*Sven Birkerts, literary critic and writer, Pontiac, MI*

I'M WITH SVEN; nothing is small. In fact there was an entire season of adolescence when I made it my private project to find the smallest object in each room, which would subsequently hold the entire universe together for me: a pencil nub, a gum wrapper on the floor, a stray smear of chalk on the board. I would choose one, then compare, or rather hold, everything and everyone else in relation to it, one at a time, to see how that changed, say, the status and demeanor of our teacher. Or the tilt of the globe. I found it softened my view of almost everyone, and everything, even and perhaps especially my own volatile moods, from whence the project itself had somehow sprung. When I wasn't holding the class star, whom I envied horribly for her beauty and tallness and thick hair and left-handedness, or the lonely kid who passed me notes I did not understand . . . if I did not hold each of these peers and the rest of the things in the room in relation to the stray marble, say, the world seemed grim. Pointless. There was no thrum, no calling, no point at all. And I was and remain fascinated by those whose posture or demeanor somehow betrayed their awareness of their relationship to the small thing; whether consciously or otherwise, some people just *knew* they existed only in relation to everything around them. Could that actually be true? And how on earth would I have been able to detect it? I would lean in toward this call of things, and how one thing seemed to hum with every other thing, then sway back out to my fixed position. Sometimes, when I was finished with whatever assignment we'd been given at our desks,

I would stare hard at something—the empty aquarium in the biology room or the fire extinguisher beside the French teacher's desk—until its form and color seemed suddenly strange, alien, as if I had never seen them before, could not imagine what function they served, and suddenly, for a few moments, the whole room would be wondrous, alive, and pulsing like static, with magic and weird atomic shimmer. This was essentially Zen practice.

Again, Joan Halifax: "Can you relax your grip on what you think is real and open your life to whatever arises? Can you see the illusion of past, present, and future? Can you let go of the reference points of solidity, identity, and separateness?"[6]

I think almost everyone lives and shifts between worlds and ways of being, for moments, for split seconds of the day, from time to time. If we're lucky—or practiced at it—we're aware of it. There's a clear or disorienting or even confused moment of so-called transcendence—and as soon as you recognize it, reify it, try to pin it down as anything other than unpredictable emergence, it is gone. Whoosh. Back not only to the apparently independent self but to the culture that aims to reinforce this independent self at every turn. Says the French philosopher and sociologist Edgar Morin, "The evils of civilization that infiltrate the soul and take shape subjectively are not always perceived."[7]

According to this invisible cosmovision (of my suburban Chicago life and now much, if not most, of the world), the universe can be explained through physical laws, evolution, and cosmology. Nothing "supernatural" happens or exists. So our crazy stories, collected here in this book, are just that: crazy stories. Fantasies. Sicknesses. Neuroses. Daydreams. Never to be taken seriously by serious people.

In some contexts, in ecological contexts, even as we inhabit this eurowestern cosmovision we can extend ourselves logically toward seeing humans as part of a living planetary system that recognizes the intrinsic value of all beings. This is wonderful where it is true. But, first, it still posits that each being with intrinsic value stands fixed and separate at some measurable, if minute, distance from all others (i.e., it is dualistic); second, this extension of scientific naturalism is not generally reflected in our systems of governance or laws (even if many individuals may intuitively agree with it). In general, we are a diverse world of diverse beliefs; and sometimes, in some places, we even give each other a good deal of allowance and freedom in articulating and expressing our respective cosmovisions and the stories that support and reflect them. Belief in the divine, for example, makes many appearances and many *kinds* of appearances in American culture and governance (e.g., there are many who view the United States as a "Christian nation" and act upon this view). But even if we allow each other some spaciousness in this regard, we don't take seriously all elements of all global cosmovisions.

There are so many constraints—both implicit and explicit—on the kinds of stories we tell ourselves and each other. If, as a person typing on her computer in a diner in western Nebraska, I say that an hour ago on a walk, my great-grandmother looked at me (she was in the form of a trembling tree branch but there was no mistaking her), that I recognized her somehow in my body and felt her presence for a split second before I registered it in my mind—what are we to make of it or of me? What if I also say that my ancestors are here with me as I type? Do I discredit myself as a reasonable person if I experience unexplainable things? Or only if I *share* them? Are there places we *can* share these experiences that don't jibe with our big shared story—our big, acceptable, and shared understanding of a eurowestern cosmovision? Ralph Waldo Emerson: "The influence of the senses has in most men overpowered the mind to that degree that the walls of time and space have come to look solid, real and insurmountable; and to speak with levity of these limits is, in the world, the sign of insanity."[8]

Ten years ago, my family gathered in Florida to accept an award on my father's behalf. He had died a few months earlier, but he had been eagerly anticipating this occasion—indeed, he was rehearsing his acceptance speech on his deathbed. Now he was gone, and we had showed up as his proxies. We stayed at a hotel that was designed to mimic an Italian seaside village, with cobblestones and Vespas parked outside, which were bolted to the ground and didn't go anywhere. In the afternoon, before the award ceremony, my mother's cell phone rang in her purse. This was unusual enough: She didn't believe in digital telephony, just as she didn't believe in the afterlife or in anything she couldn't grasp in her hand. But she took it out and saw that a voicemail had been left. It was from my father. "Hello," he said, making the word into a little song with three distinct pitches, as he always did. "I'm coming home, I'll see you soon." After she got over her initial surprise, my mother passed the phone around and we all listened to the message. We knew it wasn't a bulletin from the world of light. What happened, we assumed, was that my father had recorded those words many months ago, while returning from work on the train, and they had gotten caught in a data-storage limbo of some kind. His voice had floated around in purgatory and now, in some arbitrary fashion, it was reconstituted in our ears. Yet we kept listening to the message. It was an accident that also had to mean something. Why else had his beloved, faint, Brooklyn-accented voice been restored to us right now, on the threshold of his moment in the hematological sun, with thousands of doctors gathered in a gigantic air-conditioned hangar to pay homage, and with ten-foot-high images of his smiling face projected on either side of the podium while my sister and I accepted a handsome plaque in his stead? Of course it meant something. What it meant was that the airwaves were jammed with such sentences. They had been uttered in every language on Earth, the plosives popping and the vowels humming, and they had vanished, had been electronically orphaned, but they were still there. "So many human messages," as Saul Bellow once put it, "to give and receive." Everything we had said to each other still remained.

—James Marcus, writer, Paterson, NJ

MODERN WESTERN THOUGHT often mistakes its own cosmovision for reality itself. The anthropologist Arturo Escobar calls the eurowestern cosmovision the dominant cosmovision because there is no other cosmovision that needs to be the only one "correct" one. In his scholarship, he also calls it the one-world world (OWW; *ow!*), a term credited to John Law in his essay "What's Wrong with a One-World World?" Law argues that modern Western thought assumes there is this single, objective reality that science, politics, and economics should and can manage.[9] But this, Daishin might remind us on the nightly news (I wish he could!), is just a story (i.e., a conceptual abstraction and, I would argue, a delusion indeed). Either way, as Jane Hirshfield points out in her foreword, it isn't *neutral*. In fact, the cosmovision that seemed to be the unobserved and clean and clear water of my adolescent fishbowl—it was far from natural or necessary. It had been produced intentionally and systematically over time toward certain ends, most of which didn't really have in mind the best interests of any late-twentieth-century teenaged girl. As a matter of fact, this one-world cosmovision is not the single correct version of what we call reality—it is *only one version*. So what happens when you have an experience—the rat said thank you—that suggests the universe, and your very life, have not been adequately described by it? Do you question yourself or your inherited cosmovision?

In 2014 I had an experience with the sun—with or of the sun. It had "talked" to me in a very direct and didactic way, and I wrote down the things it "said" as I "heard" and felt them in my body. I would tell you the whole story, but I already recounted the experience, along with the things the sun had somehow "said" to me, in a book of poems called *A Sand Book* that I published in 2019.

I remember thinking that maybe I would be considered crazy for putting this experience into a book—that it could be the end of my career. (And maybe it sort of was?) I went to divinity school thinking I would try to study the history of experiences like the one I had had with the sun, and like a later one, which converged on me and a former lover—a light rushed toward us in a cornfield one night, and it stayed with us for hours, changing its shape, changing color, seeming to respond and almost even to make fun of us a little bit, here and there.

I would tell you this story, if I knew how to tell it. It's been ten years since it happened, and I have only twice told the story to more than one person at a time. I don't know how to tell it because I haven't yet figured out where the story really begins or where it ends.

In many ways my greatest struggle professionally has been to reconcile my creative efforts as a poet and playwright with the numinous dimensions of my experience. At the same time, I have struggled to integrate into my work those things that deep sorrow, alienation, and social death teach.

I have tried to find ways to make something useful for others out of these experiences, because something that I'm sure of is that being talked to by the sun and hanging out with a conscious being made of light in a cornfield—there's a long and broad history for this kind of thing. I don't think it's rare—at least it hasn't always been rare.

This past decade I've gradually collaged a kind of genealogy of theophany. For a few years I experimented with asking people relentlessly about their mystical experiences, and I thought I should maybe host a podcast talking to people about this kind of thing.

It depends what kind of a setting you're in, what people are ready to say. For a while, kundalini yoga really helped me to integrate my ecstatic experiences, because it made me feel incredible. It gradually normalized for me the possibility of feeling wonderful enough that rapturous encounters with divine love did not feel so far away from my body's realms of possibility. And meditators tended to be relaxed, open-minded, less stiff than my colleagues in the academy. It's part of why I have moved away from the academy.

But there is something not mixed enough for me, maybe, about the way insular community crops up around different aspects of identity or experience. Am I a UFO person? Am I an ascetic meditator? Am I a solitary hearer of voices, whether along the lines of someone suffering from mental illness or closer to the dazzling example of an Alice Notley?

Mostly I have been alone with what has happened to me, save the one time it happened also to the person I was with. What a profoundly romantic experience to share. And yet that encounter with the light—we used to call it the Dancing Star, among other things; we could never figure out what to call it—well, eventually it drove us apart.

I have never figured out how to tell any of this. I have seen what I've seen without dance floors, without molly or ketamine, without a ten-day silent retreat, without Burning Man. I do like psychedelics, and I visit with them every few years, and I do think they opened doors in my being.

But I found in the booming world of multidisciplinary psychedelic studies and so on this past decade or so, that the conversation often felt too materialist to me, too causal and not entangled enough—too much about dosage, replicating experience, and theories of evolution; too much about control and profit. And a lot of the art was ugly.

I went to divinity school thinking I would sort this all out. I would learn about the Hebrew prophets, the early Christians, the soma-drinking poets who wrote the Vedas. But divinity school was dry, and the people teaching those ancient texts—at least the ones I ran into—were people of insufficient Innocence, but they lacked Experience, too.

In the Blakean sense.

In many respects, dealing with what falls outside the perimeters of normative understanding has been my entire project as an artist. It has defined my life. It has named every corner and crack in my womanhood. It is why, I think, my work is often classified under the rubric "Occult," even though I am not a witch per se. I was born in Salem. I am probably witchy; something surly arises in me when I so much as contemplate the confines of traditional theology. And yet I also feel a deep and abiding love for the rigors of old-time religion. I am nostalgic for discipline and authenticity, like so many souls that feel half-starved by the treacle and slop that is supposed to satisfy our yearning for the deep, the true, the meaningful life.

What will I do with the miracles I have experienced? How can I become worthy of the blessings that have been shown to me? When I pray, these are the questions I ask.

I don't know where to begin. But this is just my starting line—I have yet to begin. I truly don't know where to begin except the occulted, maligned, dismembered, overdetermined, breathing, heaving female body. My body. Walking through the rectangular day in this rectangular city. Writing this letter in the wrong style—too dramatic, too self-serious, not plain enough, not openhearted enough, because I am so frustrated in this moment.

I used to remind myself all the time that, to the best of my understanding, Tibetan Buddhism discourages mysticism. I understand why. Sensational experiences easily become fetishes. You can get addicted to them, you can derive a wrong sense of specialness through them, you can believe you're doing "it" (whatever it is) wrong if you aren't having them.

And yet I can't quite let go of the fact that I have known bliss.

That I've experienced the sensation of being held by the divine, and I have also flung myself into living with the recklessness of one determined to be held by God and willing to be held by Nothing if only to get close to such a chance.

The ordinary human female body, and its doings, and the sensations it secretes and elaborates—my body, its true livingness, its intactness and its fidelity to my feeling, today, feels as mysterious and as elusive as a UFO, an angel, or a god. And I don't like that. I think I am identifying a problem. That the body is not just a sensory holder for the brain. That something greater than me used to help me write my poems and live my (often miserable) life. This afternoon I read about a swarm of killer drones. I opened my phone: "Should we legalize medically assisted suicide?"

I used to say to my students—it was a joke, but I was serious—that there was a conspiracy going on to make human beings embarrassed of the faculty of speech. That there was a conspiracy going on to make us so embarrassed and ashamed and afraid of speaking wrong that we would gradually give it up.

I think about children not learning to write by hand when we know the brain and the hand—our opposable thumbs—are siblings, evolving with and somehow for each other. Poets used to sing and then they wrote. Now poets hedge and hardly talk; we write complicatedly and carefully. I feel hemmed in.

I miss my body when it belonged to God. I miss my body when it was no longer a thing. I don't know how to answer the question: Have I ever experienced something out of the ordinary? Dreamed of something and then it happened? Yes, a hundred times and a thousand times.

But I think there's a conspiracy to separate me from my experience, to make me forget it, to make it hard for me to organize myself around it. And so I have failed to write to you the way I hoped to, because today I am feeling so angry and so gloomy about my own alienation. I feel alienated, like an animal playing dead.

I am glad you are gathering this kind of story, the kind I haven't yet figured out how to begin to tell.

Last year, while writing a difficult book, I got so angry about the world I stopped eating. Gradually I felt my body eating myself and I took a certain sanctimonious satisfaction in this. Eventually, though, I got sick. *That's too much suffering: Stop it,* said a voice in my head.

For several months I was cured. I no longer cried over the charred and dismembered bodies of children, I no longer wished to destroy myself on behalf of my ideals and yearnings. But eventually my body came back to normal and I cried about things in the world and in my life again. And I forgot my mystical experiences and began to feel like an average citizen, a woman who had never had a vision. I imagined buying beautiful clothes, perfecting my physique, improving my finances, organizing my thoughts. I thought about the future—not the real one, the one that's immanent always; no. I thought about a fake one, the advertising one.

The only thing that makes me feel good these days is sleep and walking through the streets till my legs are numb. I don't know anymore what I "want" but I have to conjure a deep desire soon, or I will atrophy. I remember the sun and what it felt like, in me. I remember friendship and the feeling the world depended upon our mutual understanding. I remember love, too. But I remember them today as ideas and not sensations. I remember them as knowledge, which makes me feel that I am not alive enough.

I don't know the way back through my body into that feeling of belonging to God and of restoring the world to its mouth. As I type these words, my thoughts move more quickly than if I were to write them with my actual hand, my right hand. The interfered-with cells of all holiness, none of which belongs to me, none of which is a thing—though that's what we seem to want to be lately. Even me.

I don't know. I don't know.

—Ariana Reines, poet, Salem, MA

I FEEL UNCERTAIN about my capacity to frame or comment on Ariana's words, but I can't let them hang here alone, untouched. For now, in lieu of making a bow, which you would not be able to see, I turn to the wisdom of my friend Henry Quintero—Oso, I sometimes call him—who shared these thoughts with me in another context, but they seem to me to describe the perfect opposite of the poet Ariana Reines.

> The spookiest thing is when you're among friends or with a friend and you see that they're about to make a spiritual decision, and you watch them make the decision that's safe. You watch them actually seriously disable their connection to spirit and from there on they will never be the same.

Spooky. I find it curious and wonderful that it is those individuals who *disconnect* themselves from spirit whom Henry considers to be the ghosts. Such behavior is indeed eerily unsettling. It brings to mind the character Cypher in *The Matrix*, who betrays the resistance in exchange for being dropped *back* into the matrix with his memory erased. Once there, he says, he wants to be rich, and someone famous, like an actor, who will be fully able to enjoy a steak even that, in his current state, he knows wouldn't be real. "I don't want to remember nothing," he tells Agent Smith. "Nothing." God, I can picture the actor Joe Pantoliano's face in that moment, as he says that.

It makes me wonder about the practice of turning over rocks, and what might be the ways in our world of lining them all up back into place, as if to erase one's memory of some insights or awareness. I cannot imagine what these ways would be in my own life; that old familiar ache, that pulling on the soul, would always pulse in me, I think.

Still, these experiences that don't quite jibe with an inherited eurowestern cosmovision, if not quite so bright as some of those Ariana shares—we, and I, do have ways of talking them down, explaining them away, and ignoring them. And if scholars who describe the one-world world are correct, we've probably been doing this for a long time. In *Pluriverse: A Post-Development Dictionary*, a hundred or so scholars have contributed essays to a book in which each chapter explores some aspects of modernity, their development and their crises. In their introduction, the editors describe the origins of the eurowestern ontology, tracing its roots to modernity itself, emerging in Europe since the Renaissance transition from the Middle Ages to the early modern period and consolidating into a "universal" cosmovision toward the end of the eighteenth century. It is a cosmovision defined by linear time—one in which time moves only forward and backward.[10] To this, we can add additional characteristics as described by other contemporary scholars. In a 2019 essay in *Ethics & International Affairs*, titled "Decolonizing Global Ethics: Thinking with the Pluriverse," Kimberly Hutchings describes the eurowestern cosmovision as one that considers humans the center of the world and that presupposes a fundamental separation between humans and nature, culture and nature, and, indeed, I would add, between and among all humans as well.[11] The economist Deepak Malghan writes that efficiency is its most fundamental measure of success, and "success" is highly valued.[12] The Colombian political scientist and lawyer Amaya Querejazu writes that from within the eurowestern cosmovision, all other ways of being in the world are dismissed, discredited, and/or delegitimized;[13] to this, the Canadian anthropologist Mario Blaser adds that other realities or ways of being exist only as myths or untraditional beliefs within it.[14] Finally, as my conference-going colleague told me, "Nothing about this is open to rational debate."

To be fair, many—if not most—of us do indeed consider this cosmovision to be universal—that is, it is *the* true or *correct* cosmovision. The *only* correct one. In fact, it might be *impossible* to imagine what could possibly be otherwise. If you find it difficult to envision what another ontology or cosmovision would even be, or look like, that, I would guess, is by design. (In many ways, an unconsciously designed design that involved many hands and eyes over many, many years.)

You may find you take issue with some, but not all, of these ways scholars describe a eurowestern cosmovision. Importantly, scholars who describe the one-world cosmovision in this way are not saying that modernity is bad and tradition, or something else, is good.[15] It may be easy to slip into that kind of dualistic thinking, but it should be avoided as it is simply not true. And we could generate a list of compelling counterexamples very quickly, beginning, for example, with obvious cases regarding, say, the value and importance of modern medicine, pandemic preparedness, and vaccines. Indeed, these scholars might say it is precisely the point that we *not* privilege one over the other; we can have a world of Western medicine and renewable energy technology *and* in which other ways of being, regularly experienced, are acknowledged and allowed. Surely we can all agree that ours is a universe of knowledge *and* great mystery?

Still, practically speaking, it's difficult to imagine a globalized world in which two cosmovisions coexist. It's hard to even imagine the city council of a small town making space for two cosmovisions—how practically could such a thing be done? We might begin instead by accepting that there are millions of people who live between worlds in their daily lives—caregivers, people who speak multiple languages, spiritual practitioners, people who live in borderlands of all kinds, geographical and otherwise.[16] But navigating more than one cosmovision is obviously not easy, and it remains true that in practice, in politics and across the world stage, there are many difficulties even in conceiving of political solutions and pragmatic agreements among groups with different ways of being.[17] It may even be practically impossible—as many sense and dread—to come to any meaningful solutions in time to preserve what we recognize or care about as human, as life on Earth. Perhaps this is as it should be, and "solutions"-seeking is itself an inappropriate response to polycrisis. Clearly, and in any case, we have "a long way to go toward replacing competition with cooperation," and toward replacing "winning arguments" with deeply unflinching ethical investigation.[18] Still, what an interesting line of inquiry to explore the places and people where there is already meaningful overlap, as it were. Borderlands between ways of being. What do such spaces tell us about any of the people and their cosmovisions at play? In the following contribution, the anthropologist Constanza Ocampo-Raeder, born and raised in Mexico, Grinnell- and Stanford-educated, and teaching at an elite Midwestern liberal arts college, finds herself back in her native country on ground that is simultaneously deeply familiar and unfamiliar—knowable and unknowable—and guided by human and nonhuman beings alike.

Until about five minutes before, I was feeling good about my ethnographic skills. Our guide was relaxed and explaining timber forest management with enthusiasm, proudly volunteering information pertaining to his job and impressive skills. He knew that we knew he knew. Reaching that level of trust in the rural places of this world is important if one wants to partake in what is known colloquially in my trade as community-based participatory conservation initiatives. Yet I interrupted this flow with a seemingly innocuous question: Does the community hunt here?

He looked at me surprised, a little bit *indignado* (indignant), and quickly told me it was forbidden, as this was a certified timber operation. I insisted. "¿De veras?" (Really?), I asked. "Yes!" he said emphatically, and he asked me if I had not seen all the "no hunting" signs around the entrance to trails. I had, but as we walked through this forest, the evidence of wildlife was clearly around us. Sudden shifts in the bush, musky smells appeared and disappeared, footprints, and eaten leaves. From experience I also know that game is appreciated in rural communities and that well-managed forests tend to impact game populations positively. Yet he insisted that there was no hunting, and, even further, no desire to hunt. He stiffened and changed the conversation quickly.

The forest we walk through is thick with spongy pine needles that have accumulated on the ground for years. The decaying matter smells wonderful but makes our steps unsteady and interrupts our conversations as we adjust with every misstep that sinks unexpectedly into deep concealed holes on the uneven trail. We all pretend to be professionals as we all represent different points on the spectrum of sustainable environmental professionals: local community volunteers, the community's assigned forest manager, an NGO representative, and two college professors. We have been walking a couple of hours discussing the technicalities of managing and certifying timber tree species growing vigorously within this ecosystem. Our main guide is professionally dressed—in what I call forestry chic—with cargo pants laden with bulky side pockets, sturdy boots, a hard hat, a bright vest with reflector strips, a pair of binoculars around his neck, a plastic clipboard with documents that he checks regularly, and a phone that works like a walkie-talkie as he coordinates and announces our trajectory to others. The words that dance out of his mouth are also formally attired in the language of forestry's Western ecological grammar: sustainability, timber yields, accreditation, chain of custody, DBH (diameter at breast height), environmental audits, and so on.

The conversation has a formality that feels out of place in this primeval forest that is dark, dense, and covered in epiphytes and moss dripping from the limbs of giant trees surrounding us. Yet we oblige, as we all have roles to play today. I am an environmental anthropologist—dressed in my middle-aged interpretation of a boho ethnographic look—traveling with my colleague, an ecology professor, who is decked out in Patagonia as expected. We are scouting the mountains of the Sierra de Juárez of Oaxaca for a suitable location for our off-campus studies program. Yet this is not the first human forest I have met. I have studied anthropogenic ecosystems managed by Native and rural populations for close to thirty years. I have become very familiar with the performance that ensues when Indigenous communities, in this case a Zapotec community, present their environmental ethos to outside "experts" such as us.

In these situations there is always an uneasiness as local resource managers showcase their ecological parlance in an effort to simultaneously gauge our intentions, impress us, potentially ward us off, and assess possible collaborations. (Resources can be broad in these cases and are not limited to forest materials. They can include water, wildlife, microorganismal, medicinal, and even soil resources.) In these forested mountains, the tension is crisp if still decidedly friendly. Our guide, a bright and jovial stoutly man in his late forties, has an undeniable and impressive knowledge of forest certification and the ecological attributes of this place. We are also not the first to visit this project, and his confidence is testament to the constant intrusion of outsiders from the NGO and academic realms into Indigenous landscapes wanting to learn and become inspired by participatory conservation projects. In Oaxaca, one can argue that these intrusions and exchanges have been decidedly positive, as this community combines forestry activities with lively ecotourism offerings while maintaining the integrity of an Indigenous socio-ecological landscape anchored around a milpa-based economy.

Our guide speaks effectively and with confidence, informing us about assessing the quality of lumber, managing the bureaucracy of certification protocols and regulations, and knowing the exact harvesting timetable for thousands of trees plotted throughout community territory. Yet his body is never relaxed as he declares facts and truths about the forest around us. This forest is a business, a forest to be managed, harvested, and capitalized on. He knows every tree species' name as given by a man, Carl Linnaeus, long dead on the other side of the Atlantic. He points out the habitats and habits of rare birds that bounce and chirp around the forest crevices in a way that only birdwatchers appreciate and recognize; he is also a nature guide for ecotourists who visit the area. He tells us about territorial conflicts with the neighboring community and about patrolling the forest to trap furtive collectors gathering wild orchids, moss, laurel leaves for cooking, and epiphytes to sell in local markets. He tallies up other wildlife he has encountered, calling them first by generic names such as *tigre* or *tigrillo,* only to enthusiastically light up when I ask him what kind of feline he is referencing, as this term applies to many species.

"Oh! Not the ocelot. The jaguarundi, *Herpailurus yagouaroundi.* So, you know these?" he asks. He is thrilled when I tell him how special the jaguarundi is to me: how strange their head shape is, how unexpectedly large their paws seem, how beautiful the color of their pelt is when the sunshine hits it just right. The color is an incomparable hue of gray—shiny and dull at the same time with brindle-colored tips. He agrees, and now he looks at me differently. He sees me as one in the know, and I feel the moment in which I cross the line from being a woman to be endured to one he can look straight in the eye instead of triangulated via my male colleague. This shift is hard to explain; it is an embodied experience similar to when you enter an unwelcoming room full of people who do not know you. You need to engage in a social dance that requires subtlety, testing the waters for a connection. As a woman in the field, I always sense there is a sort of misgiving surrounding my presence and have learned to identify the physical sensation of suspicion. Greetings are too quick, no one asks me why I am there, and I have to be careful about the details I volunteer about my life. In this village, the dynamics are familiar. This village is quite patriarchal, and I have been patiently waiting to break that dynamic. I have learned to purposely plot the crossing of gender lines I encounter in the field because I seek an even more profound encounter, one that cannot be paused to address superficial feminist sensibilities—one that opens up the floodgates for asking about the existence of another shared world that exists simultaneously with the one Western thought has choreographed for us. But after my initial misstep, I fear that the process may need more time.

At the end of the night we were all relaxed, enjoying freshly made tortillas and local beans accompanied by *molcajete* salsa.[19] We drank mezcal that they proudly produced in the village below. I asked if they had pulque, and they scrambled to find some; but that night they were out.[20] We were all feeling *tranquilios* (tranquil), so I ventured again to ask about hunting. Once more they reminded me, more gently this time, that it was forbidden. My colleague, a gifted Midwestern hunter, tried to elicit the information by volunteering that he not only hunted but that it was the main meat his family and friends enjoyed all year at his home. They listened, agreed that deer meat was delicious, but still they reminded us that it was not allowed and was a thing of the past. When and where they encountered the delicious gifts of deer they joyfully recalled remained elusive through the end of the evening.

The next morning we continued to trek through the forest for a couple more hours. As we reached the end of that hike, I tried a different tactic, one that had never failed me before. I asked, "Are there any *nahuales* in this forest?" I chose to ask about nahuales because Mexico, like many other Latin American countries, is a place where the human and nonhuman, the so-called real and unreal, intersect in our daily lives. (These experiences are not limited to the Americas; perhaps the most similar articulation of nahuales I have encountered happens in South Asia around encounters with djinns.) These encounters happen often but are generally unexpected; you can't seek them. When you encounter them, your body picks up on a shift. In my case, I have learned to trust this feeling and to slow down a bit to "see" with my skin. Sometimes it is a fleeting sensation as I walk by a particular tree or room or neighborhood. Sometimes it is all around you, and in this forest the feeling was intense. Not as if "someone is watching us" but instead I could almost hear an underlying buzz of otherness living, relating, and exchanging all around us.

The men were keeping track of this activity, too. I could tell as we walked through the forest because sometimes they would stop to listen to something, almost eavesdropping on fractured conversations. They were tracking nature in multidimensional ways: for other humans, for animals, for winds, for nahuales. So I asked about nahuales, and this time the men were stunned into silence. Their body language changed and their eyes opened wide with complicit smiles. Our main guide even took off his hard hat to lean in and ask me, no longer in the *usted* form but using the more familiar *tu* form, "¿Sabes de nahuales?" (You know about nahuales?)

"I am Mexican," I reminded them, "we all know about nahuales, even in urban areas."

Everyone started telling of the various kinds of nahual encounters they had experienced or heard about. The tone of the conversation was one of reminiscence, of encounters with strange yet familiar people they all knew. Nahuales are encountered in the forest, in the village, near the water hole, near the creek. They occur when people are drunk and when they are sober. When they are ill and preoccupied or when they are feeling well and celebratory. Encounters occur across the entire gamut of the human condition.

I have come to understand nahuales as liminal nonhuman beings. In common parlance, nahuales are shape-shifters known throughout Mesoamerica by different names, even if the Aztec name dominates our contemporary lexicon. Yet as shape-shifters, the exact form in which they exist is also quite fluid. Sometimes the nahual is a human who turns into an animal or an animal that acts in human ways; sometimes it is an animal that turns into a conscious spirit or an animalesque being. In some places, nahuales can be plants, even winds, if those might be known through other names. It is actually quite enjoyable to discuss the taxonomy of the shape-shifters of the world as boundaries are elusive and conversations are intricate and fascinating.

I shared my first encounter as a child with a small creature that stood in the dark next to my home's stone water filter. This nahual shifted to make its presence known and we stared at each other; it wrinkled its nose at me, and it told me it was thirsty and that the water was cool dripping out of the rock. I told it I agreed and, still thirsty, I ran back to my family to tell them. My father, a nuclear engineer, said it was all in my head but also told me that in his village, Petatlán, in the state of Guerrero, these creatures are known as *cheneques*. We still talk about it to this day; they tease me about it, but they also love telling others about my nahual, which elicits other stories from other encounters. In the Amazon during my dissertation fieldwork, I would see them often when I was walking along trails in the forest, sometimes alone, sometimes with others. We never quite talked, but there was a conversation and I knew I needed to listen; if I didn't, I would get splitting headaches that could only be alleviated by the blowing of thick, oily tobacco smoke on the top of my head. The woman that would help with my supernatural migraines would warn me to stop being so stubborn and to instead ask the nahual—or as they are called in the Peruvian Amazon, the *chuyachaki*—what they wanted. She told me they were warning me about a place or another creature and that I had to turn back or go another way to my final destination. These headaches were particular as they were immediate and intense, very different from the typical migraines I have suffered my entire life.

The men in the group agreed with me about the headaches (although you do not always get them), and so we all huddled and sat on the stumps of recently culled hardwoods to talk about nahuales. Like magic, the formality associated with the forest certification discussion disappeared. So began a lively conversation that almost immediately led to a curious declaration: "Well, yes, they are all over the forest here, and in fact, just around here there is one that we see all the time . . . when we are out hunting sometimes."

At this point I ventured further and addressed the lingering issue: "So, I thought you didn't hunt," I noted with a smile.

"Well, we are not supposed to, but people like game and we allow it if it is done traditionally."

The key word in this last exchange is *traditionally*. This word indicates the crossing of a certain kind of threshold. It is a tricky concept that changes depending on the context, contexts imposed by outsiders but also within communities. In anthropology it can be problematic if it is used to imply a nonmodern, often subsistence-based approach to doing something, so we try to avoid it unless brought up locally. In this case, the term acted like a key that unlocked permission, marking a shift in the rules under which our conversation was allowed to unfold. We could now talk about something that was taboo in another context, but I needed to be careful because hunting is delicate; it is a right that should be uncontested in Indigenous lands, but it often comes into conflict with certain dominant environmental paradigms. Instead of focusing on the issue of hunting rights, I switched my questions toward the attributes of the nahuales because those relationships capture more than hunting.

Nahuales are about connections across realms; they signal and facilitate impossible or unanticipated relationalities. Interestingly, in Mexican urban slang, you call your best friend your nahual, signaling a different kind of connection, an otherworldly connection between two beings, including two human beings. The nature of nahuales provides flexibility across realms and questions Western thought's oppositional binary imposed on the world through colonialism and neoliberalism. The role of the nahuales in society is to contest those binaries as they belong to the in-between realm of the human and the natural world. They transform themselves to mediate, and this job is literally implied in the name; the root of the word is also used to indicate "magical" transformation in Nahuatl. Nahuales mediate these relationships in clever yet unscripted ways. This liminality allows the reconciliation and negotiation of different worlds: nature-people, Western-Indigenous, subsistence-market, human-nonhuman, the objective-subjective. The in-between it reveals allows us to move effectively out of preestablished, often linear sets of social boundaries and notions of progress and into the world of entanglements. (Here I borrow the term *entanglements* from the work of both Anna Tsing and Donna Haraway. Their scholarship encourages us to lean into the complexities of the human-natural world and to avoid the impulse to only seek universal structures, order, and boundaries to explain life. Instead they encourage us to seek instances of world-making where multiple truths are able to coexist in collaboration, tension, and fluidity. The resulting chaos is where possibility, optimism, and opportunities in the future reside.) Recognizing unexpected sources of entanglements brings possibilities for new futures.

In this case the possibilities are ripe. What if the management of certified forests, a successful market-based conservation approach, included frameworks that considered the presence of and relationships that emerged with nonhuman beings? How could forest management include a more intricate consideration of cultural services intrinsic in these forests? Could cultural services be articulated in more relational terms instead of extractive terms? Current culturally inflected approaches tend to only recognize the harvest of non-timber forest products such as plants used for medicinal, ritual, or culinary purposes. What would a management scheme look like if instead of only considering harvesting cycles along timber yields they considered a mosaic of harvesting opportunities depending on the geographies established by nahual interactions? What if. We lose by insisting on solely operating within one system of being. We should not run away from entanglements but lean into these illegible complexities without fear, as they might be the source of new pots of imagination.

The next time I was back in that forest of nahuales, about a year and a half later, I once more met with a group of Zapotec men. They were all different from the previous group and once again they managed conversations through my male colleague; there was no sustained eye contact during my attempts to interact, and there was zealous reaffirmation of the no-hunting rule. In communal Indigenous lands in Oaxaca, governed under the notion of *usos y costumbres* (customs and traditions), charges for different responsibilities switch every couple of years. We had a new set of commissioners. But this time, as I walked behind the men in the forest trails, one walked up to me and asked me, "¿Usted es la que andaba preguntando de los nahuales la otra vez?" (Were you the one asking about the nahuales last time?) I said I was and he leaned in toward me and told me that there had been an uptick in nahual encounters since I had come.

To be frank, I was not sure if he meant I had conjured them up with my presence or if he was sharing a detail of forest dynamics with me in solidarity. He told me of several recent encounters and how people had been talking about them quite a bit. They were very similar in essence to the stories I'd heard before. Some included hunting, but many did not. In fact some accounts revolved around people being warned by the nahual after a behavior in the forest that was considered greedy, mostly over the extraction of a resource to sell for individual profit. Yet whether the nahual serves as a form of supernatural governance or not is not what interests me here. I think of this conversation in other terms now. In this case, I am convinced that he was not accusing me of conjuring up the nahual activity, because if you know anything about nahuales, you know that they mostly interact with kin. After all, I am not kin to anyone in these landscapes. What I do know is that this increase in activity is not out of the ordinary, as nahuales have always been there and will likely always be there. The only reason they are making themselves known now is that they, both nahuales and Zapotecs, found the opportunity—the excuse—to be in community again.

—Constanza Ocampo-Raeder, anthropologist, Mexico City, Mexico

WHAT IF, Ocampo-Raeder muses, *we lose by insisting on solely operating within one system of being. We should not run away from entanglements but lean into these illegible complexities without fear . . .*

The opportunities for collaboration in entanglement may indeed be rich. It does seem also very important to acknowledge, though, that however these entanglements might serve and support, the underlying ethic of the dominant, one-world cosmovision—grounded in dualistic thinking, including a fundamental separation between humans and nature—is the heart of a way of being that has allowed for the commodification and exploitation of nature, animals, children, and other humans, and for the kind and degree of extractivism that has led to climate change and massive species extinction.[21]

Indeed, let's circle back to this notion that we create reality with the stories we tell. Say I tell myself the story—consciously, unconsciously, or subconsciously—and from all directions hear and see it confirmed that I am separate from each and all others, separate from the floor on which I stand, separate from the boulders on the shore and the cries of seagulls and the children and wildlife starving and dying due to the armed conflict of adult humans. And that I can stand off and to the side of all of creation to study and judge the world and its other inhabitants. This "story," this cosmovision, will inform the kinds of actions I take, the virtues I either cultivate or dispense with, and the extent to which I prioritize and even define something like "self-interest." In this way, collectively, profoundly rooted in the stories of cosmovision we tell ourselves (and yes, too, in our written, fictionalized, filmed stories), I and a culture of like-minded people would find that our many, many actions strung together over time do indeed create a world. There is nothing new age or "woo" about it; it is simply a matter of cause and effect.

And likewise the other way around: If I tell myself the story and from all directions hear and see it confirmed that I am *not* separate from anyone or anything, that I exist only in relationship, that my existence and flourishing are fundamentally dependent upon everything perceptible and imperceptible in the universe, that there is no escaping this, that there is no ground upon which I might stand aside and be safe or independent from all that is, not even if I am a billionaire with a super-duper high-tech bunker . . . then this too will inform the kinds of actions I take, the virtues I either cultivate or dispense with, and the extent to which I prioritize and even define something like "self-interest." In such a way, collectively in a culture of like-minded folk, and profoundly rooted in our cosmovision, in the stories we tell ourselves about who we are, our many, many actions strung together over time might create a very different kind of world.

For some of us, it may be hard to imagine what stories based in a relational cosmovision would look like. Talking animals? Time travel? Telepathy? Actually, reports of experiencing a more relational ontology look a lot like the many stories shared in this book. Here's another, and this one is my own. May it be that in the years ahead, I am much wiser than I am now and look back and wince at this iteration of it.

~

I was living in Roskilde, Denmark, through a late spring and summer season. So when I woke up "before dawn" to meditate, the sun was already high in the sky; just as when I'd gone to bed long after "sundown," the sun was still high in the sky. I remember nothing so much about this season in Roskilde as the rooms full of light; the sliding doors wide open; the enormous wind that seemed to blow in all directions at once through the windows and stirring the tall, shaggy grass and wildflowers outside; and the sheer, ceiling-to-floor, pale-yellow curtains billowing like sails. This is the room in which I took my meditation seat very early each morning. On one morning, sometime during the hour, a magpie started calling. And sometime during that hour, the staccato notes of his cry resolved themselves into one clear, long, single note, a single syllable, as it were, communicated directly to me (emphasis on *directly*, not on *me*). If it had actually been a word, it would have been a single word simultaneously conveying reminder and caution and celebration. It was not a word, however, as the communication was, I've said, totally direct. No mediation of language required. I knew instantaneously what I needed to do. It is neither accurate nor inaccurate—and it is not at all misleading or an exaggeration—to say the magpie spoke to me. When the magpie spoke to me, the magpie was 100 percent ordinary magpie, and I was 100 percent ordinary me.

THE BIRD'S COMMUNICATION absolutely fueled me for days until, like the fading, once-searing pain of a burn on the skin, I lost its feel. And thank goodness. For the love from whence this kind of communication springs (make no mistake, it is love) is, as we all know, something practiced; it is not satisfied with nor does it clearly show itself in insights, ideas, or memories. Love is itself alive—as alive as a tree, a forest, and any of the creatures in that forest. You can never recapture or repeat an experience, no matter how powerful or seductive or life-changing it may have been, because experience always happens now. And wonderfully, the experience of love, always and only in relationship with someone or something, is always available, always at hand. No one needs to look into the past for it or be smart enough to put it into words or mental abstractions. In fact, such approaches may seriously hinder you.

And *just* now, one of my children is peeking over my shoulder at the screen, as he often does, full of questions about the changing font and the memory of Denmark. I paused and read him the paragraph above, and we chatted about it.

It's important to me that he know these stories, because we also create realities by way of stories we do *not* tell. The stories we keep to ourselves, for whatever reason. We shape reality with the stories we don't tell out of silence, shame, or even mild embarrassment. Or because the very language in which such a story might have been told has been intentionally eradicated—literally washed out of the mouths of the children who might have learned to speak it. Or they are stories that live in mysterious gaps that English and other dominant languages, for example, cannot reach. These kinds of stories just don't match up with the way we have been conditioned to perceive and understand the world: I became the coyote. The grasshopper was me. Continuity stopped. I saw myself from the dead.

I was looking back on my life from the dead, but I wasn't really me in that looking-back space. Whoever or whatever I was, I felt affection and respect for the living, human version of myself and was completely, totally released from a season of terrible depression and self-loathing. I still remember exactly where I was when this happened, the road I was driving on, the season it was, the shape of the hill I was going over, and how it felt being me and not me at the same time.

—Anonymous, Northfield, MN

STORIES AND COSMOVISIONS can be dangerous. They can incite violence, undermine authority, mobilize crowds, spread panic, challenge sacred norms . . . The wrong story in the wrong hands can distort, confuse, and mislead. The stories we tell ourselves about this world, our existence, and our place in it—whether they are fiction, nonfiction, news stories, social media stories, or otherwise—they are, again, never neutral. Perhaps you're thinking, *Really? The cosmovision that declares there is a single, objective reality that science, politics, and economics should and can describe produces stories that are empirical, secular, individualist, materialist, and modest in their claims. Is this not the very definition of neutral?*

In what most of us consider neutral stories, only humans are subjects. Some of us might be willing to grant that truth is negotiated, that reality is constituted by discourse, that there are no facts outside of interpretation, and that there is no single "master story" that everyone must use, but still—somehow, each of us stands alone and fiercely anti-bureaucratic in our own boots, defined by self-reliance and moral clarity. Myth, folktale, dreams, intuitions . . . are these not at best alternative ways of knowing the world, and are they not illegitimate because they are outdated, unscientific, and just fundamentally impossible? We *have* to restrict the stories we tell about the world because in establishing and agreeing upon rational, empirical explanations (they're not even stories, you see, they're explanations) as neutral, we can say what counts as evidence, who gets to decide, and what "problems" in our world even matter. The eurowestern cosmovision is not neutral; claiming neutrality is itself a culturally specific epistemic move. In fact, this way of knowing and being in the world is, like science itself, historically situated. It is culturally specific, it is power-laden, and it claims to be reporting the facts of reality while shaping it.[22] There are many fine scholars who have articulated this in many meaningful ways. I'm trying to channel how Daishin would put all of this—Daishin, who once told me if you can't explain something to an illiterate farmer, then you don't know what you're talking about. He was a lover of theater, and for a season of his life, an actor at the Guthrie in Minneapolis. At the end of a sitting period, after our vows, he would smile and say, "Let's strike the set," whereupon we would put away all of the props, cushions, instruments, wooden clackers, and other miscellaneous items. For him, not even in zazen—precisely not in zazen!—was there a place you could sit as if from offstage—as if you were in the audience watching something else (e.g., reality) unfold "over there." No human being could ever be afforded such a view. The *the* in theater is the same as the *the* in theory; they share the Greek root θέα (*thea*), which roughly translates to "a view, sight, or spectacle."[23] A theater was a place where people went to witness spectacle; while theory implied knowledge could be grounded in a distanced view, theory is in fact a cultural practice of viewing the object of study *as if* from aside.[24] In Zen, there is no confusion about it: It's not a spectator sport. There is no viewing anything as if from aside, and there is no background. There is no room or household task or check-cashing or dog walking to which you can't say "Strike the set." You are always onstage. If Hamlet didn't know it, Shakespeare did. And while our hypothetical illiterate farmer may not know *Hamlet,* I trust he or she would understand quite well that there's no other spring with gentler rains and warmer evening breezes from or into which the year's seeds can be sown.

What about those kinds of stories is considered by a eurowestern cosmovision to be *obviously* culturally contingent? Like experiences that are mystical? That seem to involve perception that is beyond the ordinary? That sound as if they need magic to explain them? Communicating and relating with land, rivers, mountains, animals, the dead, and artifacts that are clearly not animate? Some of these may be compelling concepts, you may be thinking, but come on; anyone telling you about an experience that is beyond the known laws of nature, that cannot be explained by science—we have a word for that: *supernatural.* And it signals one of two things: ignorance, or something that science has not yet (but will eventually) grasp.

When it comes to American Indians, there's this talk too often of "Indians and the supernatural." I can't stand it. I'm American Indian.

Consider this.

I'm in graduate school at Stanford University. What, nearly forty years ago. My dissertation is to write the life story of Mabel McKay, the renowned Pomo basket weaver and the last of the sucking doctors in California. Considered the most powerful of the medicine people, sucking doctors extracted pain and disease with their mouths. I'd known Mabel McKay since I was a young man in my early teens.

A fellow graduate student at the university wanted to meet Mabel after hearing so many of the stories I told about her. After about a ninety-mile drive from the university north to the Yocha Dehe Reservation, my friend—her dissertation was on the Renaissance—looked disappointed when an older Indian woman opened the door not in beads and buckskin but coiffed, dyed-black hair and modish glasses.

Mabel served us neatly cut tuna fish sandwiches and chicken soup, then lit a cigarette. She talked about events in and about the reservation. When she mentioned a friend she'd known some fifty years earlier who had loved a snake, my friend perked up. Finally, we were going to hear an Indian story.

Mabel's friend lived in the hills above Clear Lake with her husband. The husband had a job watching a rancher's cattle at night while they were calving, the calves vulnerable to mountain lions and coyotes. One night after the husband left for work, the woman heard a knock on the door. She was doing the dishes, and as she said to Mabel, "Something told me not to answer the door." But she did, and she found a tall, handsome man dressed head to toe in black standing before her. "Ha! I guess one thing led to another," Mabel chuckled and set her cigarette down.

When the husband came home in the morning, he found a small black snake curled in a vase on the kitchen table. He emptied the vase someplace outside the house. Four more mornings he found the black snake curled in the same place and emptied the vase. On the fifth morning he grew suspicious. "I'm going to kill it, chop it up," he told his wife. "There's something wrong here."

Panicked that by killing the snake her husband would kill the man, her lover, she confessed her transgressions. "Well then," he said, "now I'm really going to kill it." He did kill the snake, but it kept coming back nonetheless, curled in the vase each morning.

"What did this snake symbolize?" my friend asked Mabel.

Mabel picked up her cigarette. "I don't know nothing from no symbols."

"I mean was it a snake or a man?" my friend pushed.

Mabel, not hearing or avoiding the question, returned to talk of the reservation. Then a memory struck her.

"You know, not long after that, I went to the store in Middletown [near Clear Lake], and I was parked there when a man came out carrying a bag of groceries. He was tall and dressed in black. It was a hot day, summer. I watched him. Instead of walking up the road, he went down into the dry creek bed and went along that way."

Mabel started laughing. "And he was handsome."

My friend, utterly confused, asked, "Mabel, I mean, was it a man or a snake?"

"I don't know," Mabel answered, "but it was a problem."

Then this.

I'm home for Christmas. I'm an undergraduate at UCLA, four hundred miles from home in Santa Rosa. Mabel calls and asks if I would drive her up to the Kashaya Reservation to see her doctoring partner and friend, the Yomta, or spiritual leader of the Kashaya Pomo people, Essie Parrish. Mrs. Parrish isn't feeling well and wants Mabel to sing for her, to pray. It's Saturday night. I'm home from college. The last thing I want to do is drive one old woman thirty miles up a jagged coastline to see another old woman.

After I pick up Mabel—she is living in Santa Rosa—we follow the Russian River west to Highway 1. The road, everything, is socked in with fog. I can't see two feet in front of me. Even before I turn right, head north on the narrow two-lane highway, I tell Mabel, "Let's go back. This is impossible. This is dangerous."

A mile onto the highway, blinded by the fog with a two-hundred-foot cliff below us, I say again, "Mabel, we shouldn't do this. I can't see."

She hasn't said a word. She's silent, then says casually, "I knew this old woman who had a fog song."

And I think to myself, *Well, old lady, why don't you sing it?*

She hums. Chants this song. I can't remember the words. Doesn't matter. The song wasn't mine. A tunnel opens over the highway, clear to Skaggs Springs Road, where we turn into the mountains above the fog to the reservation. We park outside the old reservation schoolhouse. Mabel gets out, stops in front of the car. It seems at first that she is getting her balance. I hear her familiar chuckling, then, "I guess the song still works, don't it?"

Inside, Mrs. Parrish is lying on a bed, graying hair spread over her pillow. As I would normally do, I step out of the way so that

Mabel can make her way to the bed. But Mabel is not moving, and Mrs. Parrish is tapping the edge of the bed for me to sit down.

She watches me sit, waiting for my full attention before she says, "You have to believe these things."

—*Greg Sarris, chairman of the Federated Indians of Graton Rancheria and author of the forthcoming book,* The Last Human Bear, *Santa Rosa, CA*

ONE NEED NOT DISAVOW MODERNITY, nor be an Andean mountain dweller, a quantum physicist, or practitioner of an Eastern spiritual tradition to feel and experience resonances with a more relational way of being. All of the stories gathered in this slim book resonate to some extent with a more relational way of being. In fact, there are a lot of voices across mainstream Western culture that seem to be raising questions about the universality of a "one-world world." Again in their introduction to *Pluriverse: A Post-Development Dictionary*, the Indian environmentalist and author Ashish Kothari and his coeditors suggest that many humans, especially in industrialized countries, may feel, even if they do not ask outright: What has gone so terribly wrong with this way of living? Who is responsible for it? How am I responsible for it? What would a better life look like, and how do we get there? How can I minimize the harm I am doing? What is a life worth living? How can conditions that allow a life worth living begin to be met?[25] Philip McMichael, a sociologist and professor emeritus of global development at Cornell University, puts it most beautifully in his questions: "How is it that so much legitimate human progress seems to be betraying its promise?" and "Why do I feel so ill at ease?"[26]

In the mid-1990s, I had been functioning in the role of director of the Duke Heart Center when I was approached to apply for the chief nursing position at Duke. While I applied for the chief nursing position, it was not a position that I was appointed to. On the day that I learned that I was not a candidate for the position, I was preparing to leave for my trip to Phoenix, Arizona, since I was presenting at the Critical Care Conference there. On my flight, I thought about my career, and I realized that the role of chief nursing officer was just not meant to be for me. I have always believed that things that do not work out, for whatever reason, are meant to be . . .

At the conference, we listened to many speakers about holistic health and wellness. A guest speaker, who happened to be a medicine man, asked the audience to stand up and dance to his music as he sprinkled his healing dust into the auditorium. I felt the spiritual connection, and I understood that I would be just fine, that I would pursue a career path that was destined just for me.

That day, as the conference was wrapping up, I decided to rent a car and drive north through Sedona (spiritual vortex) and then on to the Grand Canyon. In a pair of shorts and a light jacket on a beautiful fall day, two of my nursing colleagues and I headed north. When we got to the top of the canyon, it started to snow. I didn't think much about it, until about an hour later, when I realized the temperature had dropped significantly, the sun was setting, and the snow was beginning to really stick. Since I had a rental car, without snow tires or chains, I decided we needed to hit the road and get back down to Flagstaff. Wow. The snowflakes grew larger and larger, and it became clear that as our light was diminishing, I could barely see the road, which of course had no guardrails. I went slowly, and my headlights lit up extremely large snowflakes. I assured my

friends that we would take it slowly and get down out of the canyon. I started to get scared because of my inability to see the road and I prayed silently to keep us safe. One of my nursing colleagues started crying in the back seat. It was then that I saw a large black crow come up to my window, on the left-front driver's side. It appeared that the crow was looking into the window at me. I asked my friend what she was seeing and she said, "Oh, my God! It's a giant black crow." At that point, I asked for our safety and the crow flew in front of the car, in front of my headlights. He flew left to right, in front of both headlights. I was so terrified I can't totally confirm the time-frame, but it seemed to take about thirty minutes. I can only remember praying that he would guide us out of this snowstorm . . .
I followed the crow, who continued to fly in front of my headlights until we no longer had snow on the road.

Finally, we were officially out of the Grand Canyon and moving along a long desert-type road that had no homes or businesses. All of a sudden, the crow left our side and flew to an old farmstand that read Chief Yellowhorse Produce. I stopped the car, and we all stared until our friend the crow flew away.

—Susan Whitehurst, director of Interim Healthcare (retired), Philadelphia, PA

–4–

Being Human

A human being is a part of the whole, called by us "universe," a part limited in time and space. He experiences himself, his thoughts and feelings as something separated.

—ALBERT EINSTEIN, "Letter to Robert S. Marcus"

The eye with which I see God is the eye with which God sees me.

—MEISTER ECKHART

PART OF WHAT MAKES US HUMAN is the opportunity to appreciate how much *more* we are than human. From ancient philosophers through the Enlightenment and today's most eminent physicists and physicians, not a one of us can hold out our hand and say definitively where that hand ends and the rest of the world begins. In his 2023 book *Notes on Complexity*, my friend Neil Theise, a retired pathologist of NYU Grossman School of Medicine, puts it this way: "At the microscopic level, we are thus not actually bounded by the top of our skins. Our boundaries are at least as broad as the spaces we inhabit."[1] The smaller the scale examined, Theise says, the blurrier our boundaries and the further outward they extend. At a scale even smaller than the cellular level, the molecular level, the boundary of this body of mine reaches out as far as where its molecular material extends. There is no such thing as empty space. When I stand in or across the room, I am not in it but of it. As if I were a figure made of water moving through a room filled with water. As Daishin used to tell me, "We're not *in* this all together, we *are* this all together." There is no "backdrop" or emptiness into which we can step. "At the atomic scale," says Theise, "each one of us is both our own separate self and . . . also just walking, talking Earth."

"Separation is an illusion,"[2] says Father Gregory Boyle in *Cherished Belonging: The Healing Power of Love in Divided Times,* one of his many books urging boundless love. The physicist David Bohm, it seems, would agree: "The notion that all these fragments are separately existent is an illusion, and this illusion cannot do other than lead to conflict and confusion."[3]

A fundamental question of Western philosophy asks: Am I one, or am I many? A person who experiences the world as separate from themselves—woman A from the previous chapter, for example (or Chicagoland me)—would answer that question with: "I am one. I am myself. Just as you are one. You are yourself." But, and this is so important, a person who experiences the world relationally—woman B—would *not* answer with: "I am many." She would answer, "Yes. Both. I am one *and* many."

The magpie is fully and completely and only the magpie, and I am fully and completely and only myself, and we are both also something else—everything else—which mutually constitutes us.

To such an assertion, dualism says, *Nope, sorry, you have to be one or the other—the individual person or the magpie or the many.* Nondualism says, *No problem here.* And as my own stories here, and the contributions of many others, reflect, if we can indeed hold in our awareness and even realize that we are many, this awareness does slip away. We hear this language a lot in contemporary circles: Come back to center. In Zen practice, we have to return again and again to our seat, to our attention, dropping everything, including the insights we sometimes experience in meditation. You are focused and alert, then start preparing a meal in your mind; you worry over and plan the next day's tasks. You have to come back, then come back, then come back to your actual seat, to your actual feet on the ground where your life is actually happening. It's startling to recall a roomful of meditators engaged in this practice, and to think their "coming back" to attention is like—or actually is—a practice of returning to each other second by second, moment by moment, as we recall our interdependence and mutual co-arising again and again.

Of course we cannot function responsibly in a political world or in a family or in a relationship without unique, and in some respects, separate identities—without a particular form and an apparently distinct body—that are accountable for particular thoughts, speech, and action. But it seems to me that living in this way, in bodies, requires that we regularly check each of our identities against the breathtaking mystery of existence. Dropping what we think we know of ourselves as separate or distinctive and unique beings does not mean anyone is aiming to resolve everyone and all species and forms into a homogenous "we" or "one." (It's important to note again that, perhaps contrary to popular opinion, a Zen Buddhist cosmology does *not* entail that "all is one"—that's philosophical monism, and a different thing.) What it *does* entail is a willingness to sit in the place of not knowing what it really means to be human or alive; this is a place from which empathy and compassion—caring about the experiences and fates of others—arise quite naturally.

The mid-twentieth century American Trappist monk, Catholic writer, and poet Thomas Merton reflects upon being simultaneously involved in and separated from the political and moral upheavals of his age (a position many of us can relate to). "We are already one," he writes. "But we imagine that we are not. And what we have to recover is our original unity."[4] Not just once, but over and over. Because we are not *only* "one." To appreciate this is to appreciate nonduality, the limits of a rational mind (however wonderful a tool a rational mind can sometimes be), and the wonder of being alive in a universe that is itself alive. While a person can experience being one and many—and I trust many of you, readers, have done so—it is extremely difficult to grasp this nonduality with a rational mind. A rational mind sorts and categorizes more or less dualistically, and it is wonderfully good at it. It is important to note, too, that the rational mind does not *only* sort dualistically, as many quoted scientists and philosophers herein can attest; our rational minds can and do recognize complexity, paradox, and systemic wholes. But I think it is fair to say that nonduality can be often experienced while rarely grasped intellectually. The body is a better tool for the job. The *whole* body—with its goose bumps and shaking sobs, with its laughter and ravenous hunger and need to pee; and with its apparently distant trees and leaves and rats and roaches and stars. Am I one, or am I many? It is a question that I can best contemplate with my whole body, and that whole body is perhaps bigger than can be precisely understood. At the very least, it seems, and per Neil Theise, this body extends somehow far beyond the skin of my own face and hands.

Hold in your mind again, for a moment, that grassy German hillside that Macarena Montes described, into which she and her beloved dogs Uva and Mora "dissolved."

Picture or hold in your heart as well as you can, eyes closed, the world as woman B sees it from the street corner, everything connected and in relationship.

Imagine yourself, wherever you're reading, existing only relationally in your kitchen or at your desk.

And now imagine that from above, if it were possible, a tiny swallow were to descend out of the sky, take your sleeve in her beak, then pull you upward toward the sky.

If I am not separate from you, or from the houses, trees, cities, landfills, factory farms, or wars being waged among us, then all of it—including you, and all humans actually, including our many eyeballs and everything we are seeing—would eventually be pulled up with you. Houses, trees, cities, landfills, the battlefields and all of their living and dead would be pulled up together, like a single seamless fabric, a single seamless cloth. *Everything.*

And now, if you can, hold this presumed reality for a moment . . . allow the swallow to drop the cloth from her beak, then fold herself into the seamless fabric. So, now no external bird pulling up the cloth, but all still the same fabric, or because it extends in all directions, something like a multidimensional net. You can wiggle it—the whole fabric, the entire tightly woven net; the whole universe—by wiggling your toes inside your shoes. This is not a metaphor.

It began as an unremarkable day in my professional life—no meetings, no appointments. I sat alone in my office, calmly staring at my computer screen. On it was a graph I intended to include in a book I hoped to publish. The graph depicted a familiar pattern—a normal probability curve—accompanied by an equation indicating that such patterns arise from an infinite, largely unknowable set of phenomena.

I was relaxed, almost meditative, when my gaze settled on the infinity symbol in the equation. Suddenly, a memory surfaced: something my Presbyterian Sunday school teacher had said decades earlier while trying to describe her understanding of God. Her words were something like: "We are talking about the infinite."

In that moment in my office, the symbol's meaning overwhelmed me. I whispered aloud, "My God, this is incredible!" And as I heard myself say it, the feeling intensified—my overwhelm was itself overwhelmed. A visceral sense of the infinite descended upon me. I couldn't sit still.

Turning toward the distant mountains beyond Lake Washington, I felt as if infinitely long lines were both radiating from and converging on me—in every direction. Each one was connecting me to an infinite set of things throughout all time and space. I felt at one with the universe! As Jane Goodall has said, everything "seemed to merge" with nothing ignored; no subatomic particle, no galaxy cluster, and no moment in time was neglected.

"Excited" doesn't begin to describe what I felt. I was speechless—my mind flooded with concepts beyond language, yet each one settled perfectly into place, as if it instinctively knew where it belonged. Among them was a profound sense of truth: deep veracity.

I had to leave my office; the four walls seemed suffocating. I walked along the shore of Lake Washington, where the gentle lapping of waves soothed me and affirmed what I was experiencing. I knew, with absolute clarity, that I—Chuck Fowler—was a product of the infinite universe! What's more, I realized that this was true for every being, every moment, everything—both known and unknown.

The concept of emergence suddenly made sense. I, and all beings, had emerged from reality itself. And with that realization, the nature of reality also fell into place: Reality is that from which absolutely nothing is excluded.

My walk involved a continuing avalanche of indescribable epiphanies! One simple truth was obvious: All things are interconnected—not in the way we imagine, but in the way they actually interact. Another insight followed: These interactions involve all processes—processes merely exemplified by such things as evolutionary dynamics, physical forces, chemical reactions, and natural integration. Once again, the infinite revealed its indescribable face.

Perhaps the most astonishing realization was this: What we see—directly, visually—surpasses human thought as the foundation for decision-making. During prior years, my professional work had increasingly centered on grappling with how to account for the complexity of reality. During my walk, as my mind opened to the infinite, I was struck by a profound insight: Every part of reality, every being, reflects the infinite—natural integration guarantees this to be so. We humans don't need to rely solely on our limited and biased minds to make sense of everything. Reality itself reveals what we need—through what we see.

In the intensity of that moment, I didn't realize that I was rediscovering wheels. I wasn't alone in seeing things the way they fit with one another. Later, in conversations with one of my closest friends, Larry Hobbs, I came to understand that I had arrived at ideas long articulated by the anthropologist Gregory Bateson. I also learned that in Eastern traditions, the metaphor of Indra's Net—an ancient and revered image—expresses the fundamental truth: Everything reflects everything else. And physicists, too, speak of this phenomenon, describing the universe (reality) as having a holographic presence, or memory, embedded in every part. Everything accounts for everything else; Einstein recognized this as empirical integration.

The intensity of the experience I had that day—sparked by an encounter with the infinity symbol—became a defining moment. It set the course for the rest of my life and remains an indelible part of my being.

I have since been graced with many such ineffable experiences—each one a reminder of the sacred interconnectedness that underlies all life. With each reminder I recall that day when I realized how reality permeates, infuses, echoes in, and is reflected by all beings.

—Charles W. Fowler, program leader, Systemic Management Studies, National Marine Mammal Laboratory (retired), Loup City, NE

SINCE PER THIS RELATIONAL COSMOVISION we are all part of the same fabric, since there is not a hairsbreadth separation among any of us—it is reasonable to suppose that some of "your" thoughts might somehow be accessible to "me," perhaps not verbally but in some other manner. And not in a supernatural or shocking way, not in a way that pathologizes or imbues me with magical powers, but as a matter of course. It might even be possible for two or more of us to communicate without speaking. Even spontaneously across a perceived long distance. Even in dreams. And if one of you readers were to suddenly feel a sharp pain in your back or an unbearable heartache, I too might register that pain in our shared body.

Let's extend this experiment further, pulling higher and higher on the "fabric" of a universe in which everything is mutually constituted. Eventually everything would be drawn up and everything would be miraculous. In Chuck Fowler's words, *everything*.

The piece-of-shit koan. "You piece of shit." It's one of the worst insults that can be delivered or received. I had an encounter with an actual piece of shit. You know, the way your eyes quickly scan the sidewalk or grass for those stinky landmines. I came upon said pile of excrement, as I had done thousands of times before in my life, but something about this moment, this piece of shit. Or maybe it was just residual from the LSD I did in the late 1980s or the many years of meditation, or just karma, but the shit was there, and it showed me the universe. At first I saw my aversion, the conditioned judgment and repulsion, but then there was that pause, the awareness of the social conditioning to be disgusted by it, and I was in the observer position, aware, and in the open-inquiry mode. In the shit I saw the love and care, I saw the food of the food of the food in a chain of regeneration. I saw the rain and the sunshine, the seasons that nurtured each layer of life force, from microorganisms to the insects all down the line for multiple lifetimes. I saw the soil that was created millennia after millennia. I saw the complete functioning of the digestive system, including the bacteria and enzymes and the way the body just processes it all without any conscious interference or manipulation by the thinking mind. I saw the mystical transference of energy. I saw the elements of the body, a body made up of stardust, not just of one star but many. Particles of stars that collided billions of years ago. And then I was back, standing in front of this pile of shit and I saw it as holy. Worthy of being placed on the altar and bowed to.

—Eric Manigian, designer, craftsman, and hospital chaplain, Land of the Lenni-Lenape, NJ

IN A DEEPLY RELATIONAL ONTOLOGY according to which everything is interdependent, *everything* includes what is called "yesterday" or "January 24, 1532." Pull on the fabric and you tug on the day you were born; you wrinkle last Christmas. And so, without any exaggeration or metaphor, you might well be sitting in a Placer County, California, diner while suddenly sensible of the so-called past—of everyone who had ever entered the restaurant, say, and the thoughts in their heads and the aches and pains in their bodies. Of all the nonhuman animals that fly over or scamper around the place, or who once lived on the same patch of land long, long before it was a diner or a city or even had a name. And it would be eminently possible for you to climb a mountain up the road, through the tattered clouds and way past all trees, to encounter in one split second of complete exhaustion the still point of absolute emptiness. The zero.

Augury of birds and me on the mountain with a leg that I can't move but to swing it up onto the snow, hipward, or physically manipulate it into a position bent at the knee and so hold it to drag through the surface crust that way; neither is particularly useful or kind to my body, but if I can't get down, then we'll need to call search and rescue to bring a helicopter out, and that's something I'd rather avoid, being a member of a SAR team myself and hence being mildly embarrassed at being in this situation to begin with. All the while the raven of my memory, the raven on the wind, watches with mute interest at my struggle down the mountain. What it thinks it does not say, but we all know how to understand the raven when it comes.

The rock that bludgeoned me was, perhaps, the size of a small microwave and came down in a small avalanche of smaller stones while I belayed my partner up the final scramble to the summit col on Mount Gilbert. That last bit was more a scramble than a climb, the rock all loose so that I hung back behind a corner, tied tight to the stone, letting the rope pass through the belay device smoothly as my partner went up. Near the top, a small trickle of pebbles was knocked loose by the rope, pebbles that loosened slightly larger pebbles, that became small stones, baseball-sized, and then head-sized and finally, right at the end, I watched as a great block tumbled downward, hit a stone fin, and ricocheted with a great clatter directly into my outer thigh. (My phone was in my thigh pocket and when I remove it later, it is effectively folded in half and nonfunctional. My femur, on the other hand, is intact. I have been saved a more egregious injury by Apple engineering.)

The result of the impact is a painful condition mitigated only by my carefully keeping my leg in one position or the other: either straight or bent. Moving it between the two states is impossible without a slow, hands-on manual manipulation of the leg. I can move, but only one leg will bend. I imagine that I have some kind of hairline fracture but later, in the hospital, the X-ray reveals nothing, just soft tissue damage from the blunt-force impact.

So that's the state of my life at the moment, with the immediate problem being that we're at the top of the mountain and dusk will descend sooner than we will, of no small concern since we've done this climb in a style called car-to-car, which basically means we started from the car and will return to the car when we're done, which also means that we have no gear with which to pass the night outdoors, not in temps that will be well below freezing once the sun disappears over the crest of the Sierra.

Before the darkness, though, is the current problem of the snow, for in the waning afternoon its surface is not strong enough to support our snowshoed feet, as a result of which we collapse to our waists with every third or fourth step. It is miserable traveling. At some point I simply roll across the snow like a dog, pulling myself over with my ice axe, flopping over, doing it again. This is no better way to travel and I would not recommend it, but it is, for the moment, the only real conveyance I have. Three fingers on my right hand are numb and my glove there is shredded from dragging it through the snow crust over and over again.

My partner waits for me whenever there's any kind of step down, as I only have the one bendable leg. I put my hand on his shoulder and lower myself and grunt and moan. He's being a good sport through it all, although I can also tell that his stress level is rising. If I get caught out here in the dark, then so does he, so he tries to get me moving with some speed. At one point we realize that we've gone down the wrong side of a ridge and have to backtrack to the top and descend the opposite side. He is fiercely apologetic, but I am resigned to my fate. We'll either make it out of this before dark or we won't.

On the way in, we'd talked of his parents, who he describes as an old Jewish couple who do not understand why their son is interested in alpinism. All climbers have had these conversations; the draw of the mountains is not easily articulated to the sane. Not in this language. But there are others, of course.

During that conversation we were headed up a great broad bowl of snow. Somehow I was in the lead—a rarity since my partner is half my age and twice as fast—and when I turned back to look at him, it was to find a raven hovering just behind. "There's why we do this," I said to him, my partner, not the raven, or maybe indeed to both. My partner turned and looked and soon we were both there, looking, the raven peering back, saying nothing but simply floating on the wind just a few feet above the surface of the snow. And then it was gone, angling its wings and drifting away. *Okay,* I thought, *so this is gonna be one for the books. I'll keep my wits about me. A warning,* is what I thought. A warning to be mindful.

But now, stumbling down the mountain with my injured leg, exhausted, darkness descending, frozen to the bone, my body tells me what my thoughts got wrong. I feel not so much some anthropomorphized cartoon raven warning me to be mindful but instead the inscrutable and impossible and bridgeless gap between species, and in my awareness of that gap, the gap closes.

It is not magical. It is mundane. It is magical.

There is no augury of birds. There is only an augury of birds.

And stone. And snow.

Such is my experience as I roll down the mountain, break through the crust, cry and moan and weep with fatigue. We make it back to the car just as the sun disappears and the world is plunged into darkness. I almost weep with exhaustion. My partner slumps into the seat. "I'm wrecked," he says. From somewhere out there in the new night, the raven calls: *Krraak. Krraak.* I know what it means. I'll never know what it means. I know what it means.

—Christian Kiefer, professional bleeding heart, Los Angeles, CA

IT'S NOT BY ACCIDENT that Christian had this experience when completely physically, emotionally, and mentally exhausted. It is not just for the sake of rigor that in a silent Zen retreat, we rise early (at Great Plains Zen Center, it was sometimes a 3:50 a.m. bell) and sit not once but over and over and over again, eating just enough highly nutritious food at regularly placed meal and snack times to sustain us until lights-out after 9 p.m. "What is the meaning of Zen?" a student asked Master Hsiang Lin, the tenth-century Chinese Zen teacher. "Sitting long and getting tired!" the master answered. Fatigue can dissolve much of the persistent looping thought of the intellectual, discursive mind, which may allow experiences such as Christian's to be noticed, if not also deeply felt. That discursive mind likes to chew, and it is so good at it, so masterfully good at it, it will chew in a way that convinces you it is not chewing.

My friend Anne Fernandez, who had been practicing meditation for some years, finally experienced a breakthrough soon after. All in less than a two-year period, she got married, had two babies, and moved away from her family to take a rigorous and full-time academic job. She was, in a word, exhausted.

Even buoyed by this profound parental love, daily life was unrelenting . . . The lack of control I had over my own life struck me in a way it hadn't before. I wanted to laugh and cry in frustration at the inescapable obligation of parenthood, but there was nothing I could do and no one I could cry to. Instead, I mentally surrendered to and experienced a sense of freedom and acceptance that rearranged the puzzle pieces of my life. Another layer of selfishness and egocentricity sloughed off me without my permission.

Looking back, perhaps it shouldn't surprise me that these events would change me in other ways as well. In my twenties I practiced meditation regularly, after picking up *The Miracle of Mindfulness* off a friend's coffee table. I expected this book to peddle hollow new age affirmations, but instead it contained profound practical instruction on the importance of paying attention. I subsequently learned more, attended meditation retreats, did a few stints in Zen monasteries, and pursued a doctorate degree that involved studying mindfulness and addiction. Yet my meditation practice was marked by struggle and striving. I stopped meditating for the better part of a decade.

Eventually the pressures of new parenthood caught up with me again. After my second child, a beautiful baby who woke up at night every two hours, I found myself again an exhausted husk of a human. On a whim, I decided to return to meditating. With little fanfare or expectation, I began. I sat multiple times a day, every day. It was as simple as the words I read so many years ago. I just paid attention, too exhausted to do much else. It was postpartum-induced "beginner's mind" in the Zen nomenclature. My mind was an open room, thoughts and sounds floating like dust motes in the sunlight. It was simple, powerful, pragmatic, and transformative.

—*Anne Fernandez, licensed clinical psychologist and professor of psychiatry, Newport, RI*

WHEN WE EXPERIENCE the self as empty in the way that Anne describes, the better we sense the radical extent to which we are all pulsing with that aforementioned atomic shimmer in a complex choreography beyond intellectual understanding. The better we sense the seamlessness of the fabric.

Thích Nhất Hạnh has a wonderful name for this seamlessness: interbeing. As in, you and I inter-are. As in, nothing and no one exists in isolation, no matter how lonely that imagined Archimedean point might feel. As in, none of us has a fixed or separate self but comprises elements and energy that temporarily hold themselves together in a certain form, then take another form . . . And if you take hold of your own thumb or caress the face of your lover, there is literally no knowing how many others you are touching, nor how the effects of your touch may be felt, nor how far, in space or in time. What if it matters the way you touch everything that you touch? "All that you touch you change," writes Octavia E. Butler. "All that you change changes you."[5]

The late Thích Nhất Hạnh—or Thay, as his students called him—"has given us all of his life," Egyoku Roshi recently shared in a teisho. "He lives in us." Surely *this* is a metaphor?

I dreamed I was at Tu Hieu Monastery in Hue, Vietnam, where Thích Nhất Hạnh lived, taught, and passed away. Every morning I saw him walking, sometimes even running, as if the dream were gifting me impossible images of his daily life—Thay in the gardens, in the woods, always in motion.

Suddenly I was kneeling before him in a garden. He placed his hand on my forehead and offered me refuge. As I received it, a powerful current ran through me—it felt like dying and being reborn at the same time. When I came back to myself, I was walking beside him. I wasn't a nun, but I accompanied and cared for him as if I were his assistant.

I remember a large hall with mosaics, fountains, families, children running around, and even my dog Chapulina among them.

Thay sat at a table with my friend Joanna, talking while I joyfully immersed myself in the water before waking up.

This dream was an initiation, a blessing—something I hope never to forget. The whole next day, I felt him with me, as if I had received his direct refuge, actually. The dream has stayed with me in a way that feels very different from a regular dream. It didn't feel symbolic or distant—it felt like a direct encounter. All the next day, I carried a sense of presence, as if Thay were walking with me, quietly guiding me from within. The refuge I received in the dream left a physical sensation, a kind of energetic imprint, like a blessing that keeps unfolding.

—Ximena Romero, cocreator of Restaura Experience, Néctar, and IKAL Tulum, Mexico City, Mexico

NEUROSCIENTISTS HAVE MADE startling and wonderful discoveries about the human brain and dreaming. (Among them, I love the scientific confirmation that the brain accepts impossible scenarios as real.) In addition, many neuroscientists agree on what we *don't* yet know: what dreams tell us about consciousness; why consciousness persists during REM; why dream consciousness feels so real despite disconnection from the environment; why dreams take the form they do; what any evolutionary purpose of dreaming might be; why dreams are so bizarre; why the brain seems to invest so much emotional energy in dreams; or why some dreams feel so meaningful. I too have had these dreams that feel like visitations. One of my fiction teachers, Ron Carlson, once told me that the entire point and purpose of dreams is to visit the dead. This is a notion that seems on its surface to be kind of lovely, but which on a deeper level is wise and mysterious; there have been many days and seasons when I have agreed wholeheartedly with Ron on this point, and I do wonder how much the insight has to do with neuroscience's aforementioned unanswered questions.

My older sister and I have had variations of the same recurring dream since childhood. I discovered as a teenager that whenever I dreamed of swimming, I actually held my breath. I have a totally unfounded belief that there are two kinds of people in the world: people who have flying dreams and people who don't. I have had many lucid dreams and kinds of lucid dreams, and I love talking about these with my children, who are always shocked and wonderstruck when in the morning, one of them recalls being aware of one of the night's dreams as a dream. I have had many dreams in which I have the presence of mind to begin zazen, which opens up very strange and visceral experiences and storylines indeed. And I have had the great good luck to work closely for many years with a Jungian analyst; the mystery and richness of our dreams are storehouses of treasures, however you look at them.

My know-it-all smartwatch tells me that I spend roughly the same amount of time in dreamlike (REM) sleep as any other human, but I remember almost nothing about the dreams I am supposedly having. I am surprisingly at ease with this quirk of my brain's wiring. It makes the rare dreams whose fractured remains survive the transition to my waking moments all the more memorable.

Recently, while on sabbatical in Jamestown, Rhode Island, one dream vividly smashed its way through the sleep-wake barrier. I was standing in a skybridge, with bright and subtly refracted light pouring in through a patchwork of DNA-shaped lenses embedded in the bridge's glasswork. A nondescript entity stood in the light but, like everything else in the dream, cast no shadow. It said, "Bison evolved an additional pathway connecting their left and right brains" and provided very specific details about the neurons involved in this pathway. Exhilarated and awoken by these words, I immediately said something akin to "You're not going to believe this" to my wife and proceeded to describe and also write down everything I could remember.

Why did these otherwise random, mundane words elicit so much wonder? I run a neuroscience research lab, and a few months before the dream, we had serendipitously discovered that the left brain and right brain play a game of rapid neural ping-pong that goes into overdrive during dreamlike sleep. Neurons in the left and right brain start volleying information back and forth to each other at a remarkably high rate of knots, but also with exceedingly high precision. Perhaps this is when our neurons try to replay and make sense of our waking life, synthesizing snippets of our actual experiences with loosely related concepts and emotions, giving rise to the dreamlike perceptions that lie at the tantalizing boundaries between sense and nonsense, meaning and confusion, fascination and fear. This is conjecture, though. Neuroscience does not yet fully understand how our neurons sculpt the contents of dreams, why we remember some dreams but not others, why dreams can occasionally unmask awe-inspiring levels of creativity or insight.

What did I make of my own dream? I was disappointed with my subconscious self for not assigning shadows to the objects in the dream. Perhaps it would have done so if I was an optical physicist or an oil painter and light and shadows mattered to me as much as neurons and memories. Of course, it's very possible that it wasn't my unconscious brain forgetting to add in the shadows but my conscious brain choosing to remember the dream content with this shadowless filter and blaming the other me, even though that other me was using exactly the same neurons as my conscious self. I'll never know for sure. The skybridge was a fantastical version of one that I walked through thousands of times in graduate school. And what about those bison brains? As I dug into understanding the words from the dream, I realized they were remarkably accurate: There was indeed a second prominent set of neurons in mammals—including bison and humans—that connected the left and right brains in very precise ways. Those words helped me start a research project focused on figuring out exactly which of these multiple neuronal pathways connecting the left and right brain give rise to the game of neural ping-pong, a project that we are now close to completing.

Our brains did not evolve to be perfectly rational or perfectly logical. They did not evolve to detect the objective truth: They cannot resist the lure of a seductive lie repeated over and over again. They did, however, evolve to attach meaning and make sense of the world around us so that they can inform our next decision and guide us on our next journey. They are doing exactly this even as we sleep. My own sleeping brain played a game of neural ping-pong to make sense of how it could be playing a game of neural ping-pong.

—Omar J. Ahmed, neuroscientist, Karachi, Pakistan

A dream I had the other night brought all this to mind. It's the most obvious business on the face of it, far too direct but a place to start. Lynn and I were watching one of our nightly crime shows when I remarked, as I do all the time, that an actor on the screen reminded me of someone we both knew. "That actor reminds me of G," I said. She didn't see it at all, and I didn't belabor it. But—no surprise—I had a vivid dream that night in which G and I were in on something together, easy, in cahoots, like we'd known each other forever. The face on the screen had triggered me.

G and I had known each other for several years. We had taught in the same writing department; we had taken delight in literary gossip of all kinds. We were both ambitious. Some years later, we were faculty in the same low-residence writing program, lived together in a faculty house; we once team-taught a workshop together. I would say we were friends.

But things move on. We haven't been in contact since the early 2000s. Our ambitions took us in different directions. I became a book critic; G engaged in larger issues. He would often show up as a guest on some of the news shows we watched.

My point is not that he appeared in my dream but that the dream seemed to come from a deeper place than my memories. It had us in some situation I've already forgotten, but it also drew on a familiarity we had never quite reached. The dream felt full of meaning and was imbued with an urgency of mission. I woke up with a warm feeling, certain of a depth that nothing in my memory warrants. Yet—this is the strange part—I had the sense that our way of relating in the dream was the truer story. It's happened to me a few times before, my dream creating a sense of intimacy with a person that's richer than what I remember, as if it's one of my other lives that I'm momentarily tapping into.

—Sven Birkerts, literary critic, Pontiac, MI

I HAVE RECURRING NIGHTMARES, too, from which I wake myself up calling, shouting, even crying (it happened once when I was rooming with an unknown scholar at the Dickens Universe in Santa Cruz—sorry about that, roommate). In many nightmares, I have a sense of evil very nearby, and as it approaches in its various dream forms, my body begins to prickle with heat and something like horror, like my body is nothing but static and the electricity in it is getting supercharged. And at this precise moment, for as long as I can remember, I start in my dream to sing the Lord's Prayer. And it always,

always fends off whatever is coming for me. It doesn't matter how many sutras I memorize—in my nightmares, it is the Lord's Prayer that saves me.

I once recited the Lord's Prayer in Spanish at the wedding ceremony of a very dear friend, the poet and writer John Olivares Espinoza. I was very moved to receive this contribution from him and to know that we live together in more ways than the one inside this beautiful and ancient prayer. It feels important for me to say, too, that I'm not at *all* sure what he is describing here was a dream. Or if it was a dream, what a dream is.

It happened to everyone in my family. Mom. Dad. My big brother, too. Uncle Jesse not long after he arrived from Mexico. At sixteen I wanted it to happen to me so badly. It happened so often to my family we had a phrase for it: *Se me subio el muerto*. The best I can translate is "the dead got on top of me."

I dared the dead to use me as a mattress. Proof there was something more wondrous than the life I led. Every now and then we heard something odd in our house. To hear a ghost was bull. Seeing a ghost would not do either. I wanted to feel one. Live through the terror. Recount it like a nightmare the next morning while stirring coffee, like my mom and dad did. Saturday nights I slept on the living room sofa. Some nights I awoke to the sound of the house settling. Most nights I slept soundly.

My little brother and I shared a room. I slept in a full bed and he slept in a twin flush against the wall. We never talked about *el muerto* in front of him as not to scare him. Two or three nights into the week I returned home for winter break after my first quarter of college, I was awoken by the feeling of someone climbing on top of the foot of my mattress. I thought it was my little brother seeking refuge from a bad dream like he would when he was little. I turned toward his direction expecting to see the sheets pulled away from an empty bed. My brother was there sleeping soundly.

Immediately I felt a dense weight come on top of me. It felt like the weight of a person three times heavier than me. I turned my neck to call my brother for help. No amount of effort could get me to speak. What I saw next I never understood the why. My brother rose up from his bed and reached out to me. Except he was entirely colored in red. His hand, his arm, his face agape in terror. The sight injected so much fear into me because whether or not I was experiencing a dream, I knew I was going to go at it alone.

No more than a second had passed. I could not speak. I could not move. If I could breathe, I could not tell because whatever was on me compressed my chest. I felt the presence of a head next to mine. The desire to push this thing off me was there, but even my fingers were pinned to the bed.

Another second passed. Fully awake I noticed an opening in my ceiling. A dark upside-down funnel with a wide mouth. It churned. Inside, shadows swirled. Faceless, limbless, shapeless shadows. They swirled inside the funnel inside my ceiling. Then the worst. One shadow swooped down at my body. It tried to strike me while this thing laid on top of me. When nothing came out of its attack, it returned to the funnel with the others. They took turns. One after another, they swooped down from the funnel at me, returning to the swirl after each attempt to do whatever.

Meanwhile, I'm more scared than I had ever been in my life up to that point, paralyzed under the weight of el muerto. The only defensive and offensive measure against evil, I was raised to believe, was prayer. Jesus to the rescue. Jesus, whom I turned my back to the last ten weeks by drinking to excess, skipping Sunday Mass, and worst of all, my participation in summoning the spirits with my friends in the dorm hall lounge with the Ouija board. Faster-than-a-speeding-bullet Jesus. Jesus, a real American hero.

I started to pray in my head. "Our Father, who art . . ." I didn't get very far. "Our Father, who . . ." I repeated the same opening words. Starting and stopping. Repeating "Our Father, who art. Our Father, who. Our Father, who art in." I was trying to radio the Lord and these things were jamming the frequency. Hope crumpled under the futility of prayer as I thought, *It's not letting me pray. It's not letting me pray.* I couldn't move. I couldn't talk. I couldn't remain in this state of terror until sunrise. I rationalized that if these malevolent spirits scrambled my thoughts of prayer, it had to be for a reason. It felt like trying to read text in a dream, but I pushed through and I pushed back until I got to the very end of the Lord's Prayer.

The invisible weight on me dissipated. The ceiling became quiet. Breath entered and left my chest. I turned to check on my brother. His back was turned to me in undisturbed slumber. The experience must have lasted a minute. I continued to pray in my head until I fell asleep.

Awakened hours later by the sound of my mom stirring a spoon inside her coffee mug, I came out to the kitchen and said to her what I often heard her say to us: "Se me subio el muerto anoche." Nothing in my story gave her doubt. As time progressed, I thought about whether a ghost had really taken possession of my body or if I dreamed it all. Later I would learn about sleep paralysis and how my experience checked off every symptom. So that could be another name for this experience that I lived, fought through, and survived. Whatever you call it, however you understand it, it happened to me.

—John Olivares Espinoza, poet, writer, and manuscript consultant, Indio, CA

SEVERAL YEARS AGO, in Minnesota, I was paged to meet with a fifty-five-year-old patient who minutes before had received a stage 4, inoperable cancer diagnosis. She had come to the ER several hours earlier assuming she had a badly pulled muscle and was otherwise in good health. What she took for groin pain was the symptom of an otherwise silent disease. She had recently moved back home from Montana to live with her mother, after having an ominous and very clear dream that she would need to be in her mother's house to support a death. Her mother was in her late eighties and lived alone, and it made sense on many counts for this patient to rent out her current home and move a state over to be with her mom through the end. "But it was me," the patient told me. "It was me who I dreamed about." Amid shock and fear and devastation, she was wonderstruck. "Who inside of me," she asked, "was looking out for me in that dream? Or was the dream not inside of me?"

–5–

Storytelling, and Storytelling

Digressions, incontestably, are the sunshine; they are the life, the soul of reading!

—LAURENCE STERNE,
The Life and Opinions of Tristram Shandy, Gentleman

THERE ARE MANY HOURS AND DAYS in our lives in which, without ever explicitly announcing itself, the dominant Western one-world cosmovision describes the universe and our place in it with quiet authority. When it functions in this way, the extent to which it shapes and prescribes our actions is enormous precisely because it does so invisibly. The stories we tell and the stories we believe, as well as the stories we do not tell and cannot quite believe, are shaped by the cosmovisions we inhabit and, in turn, help perpetuate them. This was true of the stories once told around the fire, and it remains true of the mainstream stories now delivered through paperbacks, films on airplanes, television, literary quarterlies, and workshop manuscripts passed around a seminar table.

As a novelist, student of literature, and erstwhile creative writing student, I'm curious about how these mainstream stories (literary fiction very much included) and the "workshopping" of them stabilize one version of a single kind of world. I appreciate that my questions are enormous and that in this single chapter I can address them only as hunches and worries. Is it right that, and worth considering how, one dominant kind of narrative authorizes what kinds of being exist, what being is like, and what kinds of relationships count as real? These questions are spiritual, too, insofar as they involve not only questions regarding what a self is in theory but what kind of being one experiences oneself to be. Not only what worlds stories represent but what modes of attention, relation, and reality they cultivate; not only how narrative organizes causality but what it permits us to recognize as meaningful, alive, or sacred.

I was always attracted to eighteenth-century prototypical novels both because they are so wild and messy (it's so obvious to a modern reader what is "wrong" with these early books, and every apparent glitch raises dozens of questions), and because before academic disciplines were separated and codified, they were a privileged site for working through crises of being and knowing of all kinds: What is a self? What's it made of? Does it persist over time? Is it rational? Autonomous? Theatrical? Is it ever complete? Where does one self end and another begin? Authors of these books raised such questions in narrative forms that can be tracked with some clarity for a student of literature. And while these are philosophical questions about personhood and literary questions about characterization, they're also spiritual. They concern the lived reality of separateness, interdependence, identity, dissolution, what kind of being a person is, what kind of world this is, what counts as knowledge in it, and how one ought to inhabit it. In works of fiction, these become formal questions about narrative authority, motive, interiority, temporal sequence, the relationship between experience and legibility, and so on. Authors of "early novels" didn't assume personhood—whatever it was—could ever be narratively described or secured. They worried it, expanded and contracted it, parodied and pilloried it, and self-consciously failed to contain it. And they are wonderfully strange—far stranger than the later literary histories that recruit them into a tale of formal development.[1]

Laurence Sterne's *The Life and Opinions of Tristram Shandy* and Samuel Richardson's *Clarissa*—sitting ducks, to be sure—don't develop reliable techniques for representing interiority or selfhood but expose willfully, and perhaps accidentally, how precarious an exercise it is to represent a self on a page. With elegance and in mischievous play, Sterne totally sabotages the premise of a life told through sequential reports of a coherent, independent self. Richardson seems at first to secure personhood through epistolary interiority, but the opposite happens: He gives us a self that proliferates across letters, that is distributed across correspondence, misread by others, claimed by competing moral vocabularies, and progressively overwhelmed by the very social forms that seem to record it.[2] (I have read the unabridged *Clarissa* only once, because life is short, from a folding lawn chair on a grassy yard through a long stretch of blue afternoons in Wyoming. It was perfection in every possible way, and I just wept and wept.)

In graduate school, I was obsessed with a kind of disgusted admiration for Jane Austen, who matters profoundly amid these questions. Whether she intended to resolve the ontological uncertainty of her predecessors, it sure feels like she does—and in her fiction, the "settling" of many philosophical questions become newly and powerfully authoritative. She arranges consciousness, motive, narrated action, and social legibility so elegantly and with such control that it's easy to mistake for nature. And easy to want to reproduce. I find it wonderful fun to search her novels for gaps or glitches in the elegant, reproducible machinery, each of which, in my view, betrays perhaps as much mischief as Sterne had up his own sleeve. In Austen's wake, you can almost viscerally feel consolidating the model of an intelligible person whose inward formation can be rendered with subtlety, whose motives can be inferred without too much overt statement, and whose choices can carry the burden of plot. This arrangement becomes enormously consequential because it later passes into pedagogy as if it were merely craft rather than a historically specific way of narrating a person and a world.[3]

I learned one version of this history-disguised-as-craft pedagogy in creative writing classrooms in the early 2000s, where it was never remotely presented as history but as inevitable and publishable common sense. I was studying the "rise" of the novel alongside attending workshops, however, and doodled in the margins of Nancy Armstrong's *Desire and Domestic Fiction* a little acronym to express the formula for writing fiction as I was piecing together: EPiC MAP. *Exposition* (a person's past) gives rise to *psychology*, and their psychology gives rise to *character*. Character gives rise to *motive*, and motive gives rise to *action*; action, strung together, creates *plot*. Not always strictly linear, but close enough. I kept seeing the same structure under different surfaces: realist domestic fiction, literary historical fiction, speculative fiction, even novels that in many ways seemed resistant to formula. The world could be bizarre, the sentences dazzling, the chronology disrupted, but the basic engine was so often—and startlingly—the same.

What struck me was that EPiC MAP was not merely a plotting device. It was a compact metaphysics. It presumed a particular kind of being: a bounded person (separate from everything around them) whose interior organization precedes and explains action, whose relations to others and to the world appear mainly as pressures, contexts, obstacles, or occasions. When this model is used, relation is secondary. Other beings, systems, and worlds matter chiefly insofar as they impinge upon or are interpreted by the character. Aesthetically, EPiC MAP can do many things at once: organize plot through inward causality; stabilize the self as the privileged bearer of coherence; subordinate relation to already formed individuals; translate world, system, and setting into inputs for a character; and naturalize all of this by presenting it as narrative competence rather than as a theory of being.

I've not taught creative writing in a long time. But back in the day, the students I had who wanted to "be writers" intuited this formula for realistic, character-driven fiction or had it directly described to them; they more or less diligently set to work writing stories and novel drafts, and they did well. Those in class with the mortal wound, as it were—they looked at me skeptically. Can we break those rules? Can we not do it differently? Or even: That does not really fit with my experience of being alive or with what is calling me to create art.

If you've spent time in workshops, you know which spirits I mean; their work is often hard to read or follow. It doesn't make sense to many of us. The best of it we may call weird or magical—of a different genre perhaps. In the worst of it, we see an unpracticed writer but good thinker who has had little or no guidance or experience regarding any other sense of self, way of being, or relationship to story, only an intelligent hunch that something is off about how they're being taught to represent reality in a fictional way on the page; who, instead of writing what they know, try to write what they *don't* really know but sort of do, or wish they did. They get carried away by using their intellect to fill the gap—and this stuff is often unreadably bad. So, it's situational. Sometimes, what doesn't conform to this underlying, mainstream aesthetic is called "experimental." Another former creative writing teacher of mine, Percival Everett, used to say the most "experimental fiction" of all was realist fiction. He's right, of course; but it works a lot like a cosmovision that we can't see as cosmovision. Whosoever calls good realist fiction a successful exercise in verisimilitude is demonstrating the point.

But I, too, like some of these aforementioned students of mine, find so many of the "answers" to so many questions about being and knowing the nature of the self in relation to the rest of the world—as these "answers" are presented aesthetically in many stories, novels, and films—to be hollow and unsatisfying, even if captivating and seductive. While such formulations of selfhood may significantly, if not completely, free me from many sociopolitical prisons, it does not really describe my experience of being in a body or in a world.

(Relatedly and importantly, we could fill a whole other book with contributions from people regarding experiences of this "self" falling away in moments or activities of great absorption and attention.

Curiously, many of us may experience this when immersed in, say, one of those exquisitely penned Jane Austen novels.)

The clearest proof, in my view, that EPiC MAP is not just a complaint about bad or schematic fiction is that one can see its logic at work in novels that genuinely are some of the most truly timeless and beautiful works of literature. In George Eliot's *Middlemarch*, Dorothea Brooke's moral imagination and psychic formation generate motives that make her choices legible and thus produce plot; the novel is too intelligent to reduce her to mechanism, but it still depends on inward coherence as the medium through which event becomes intelligible. In Ian McIwan's *Atonement*, Briony Tallis's early habits of perception, order, and interpretive confidence harden into disposition, and that disposition produces the action on which the novel turns. Metafiction does not abolish the chain from formation to action but rather exposes its power and its danger.[4] Of course, these and hundreds of other wonderful novels I love are not reducible to formula. That's the point: The formula names a deep grammar of mainstream intelligibility, not a defect of inferior writing. The formula is mesmerizing.

Sometimes, no matter the nature of the story, the beauty of a single perfect sentence alone strikes me as a living thing, humming with all the energy of a tree leaf or a bird. So this is a major exception to all of these questions about aesthetic form, the lifeblood of language itself: Even a single, perfectly placed verb can momentarily dissolve all the boundaries between my own edges and the world "around" me. (I was just rereading Ron Hansen, this morning, whose sentences have this effect for me on almost every page.) Further, there are of course many artists who have that aforementioned "mortal wound." These are the humans whose ache has no cure, but who, seeking medicine, nevertheless continually push every edge of artistic possibility. Virginia Woolf, Toni Morrison, W. G. Sebald, Ali Smith, and many others—their work complicates any too-neat story about realism, inwardness, or narrative legibility. They stretch scene with essay, braid self with history, let voice exceed person, and make relation, memory, atmosphere, and the more-than-human press upon form in ways that do not sit comfortably inside any version of aesthetic "common sense." As modes of storytelling, of course fiction and the novel have always contained insurgent possibilities; may it always be so! But I do not think these counterexamples make my underlying questions disappear. If anything, they sort of clarify it: One feels the force of such work precisely because it pushes against inherited expectations about what counts as coherence, plausibility, motive, and reality on the page. Not all fiction obeys the model I'm describing—of course not—but the model seems dominant enough that departures from it register as departures and are sometimes characterized as "difficult" because they do so.

But while I'm at it, and because I still hear and see this imperative all over the place: "Show, don't tell" is related in important ways to the EPiC MAP formulation.[5] "Show, don't tell" is the more visible craft directive: Dramatize rather than explain; imply rather than declare; trust scene, gesture, detail, inference. EPiC MAP operates underneath it as a model of what kinds of beings and causes plot is supposed to consist of; it organizes plot by inward causality. "Show, don't tell" *naturalizes* that causality by making it *appear* scenically discovered rather than conceptually imposed. And indeed, if a narrative already assumes that persons are coherent interiors from which motive and action proceed, then "show, don't tell" becomes the ideal machinery for making that chain feel discovered rather than imposed. Rather than naming a theory of selfhood in any expositional way, the prose gives us habits, speech patterns, gestures, memories, and decisions from which a reader is invited to infer a deep interior structure. This can be wonderful. As a reader, I'm trained to become a detective of interiority, treating habits, gestures, speech, belongings, and actions as clues regarding a hidden structure of selfhood. I experience this as discovery, not construction. But this pleasurable process assumes there's a deep interior structure to find and that a self can be known through careful inference. When I read, how often am I practicing the ontology of the one-world-world and experiencing it as pleasure? Does the cosmovision reproduce itself not only in what stories say and how they're said but also in the very activity of reading them?

And so do the ontological assumptions disappear into method. This is one reason the rule to show, not tell, has seemed so natural for so long. But historically, this naturalness is produced, not given. Scene, sensory detail, inference, and distrust of overt explanation became dominant through a lineage running from Jamesian scenic method through Percy Lubbock's codification of point of view and into postwar American programs and craft handbooks.[6]

What troubles me, then, is not only that "show, don't tell" mistakes one narrative mode for narrative itself (which it does by elevating scene above other indispensable narrative modes: summary, exposition, reflection, commentary, digression, direct judgment).[7] Rather, it is a deeper problem. "Show, don't tell" naturalizes a very particular theory of reality: that the real is what looks unmediated. (Talk about an aesthetic that doesn't jibe with my lived, bodily experience or my call to create art!) The more a narrative suppresses overt explanation, historical framing, authorial judgment, and conceptual linkage, the more "real" it can appear. Mediation of any kind starts to look like contamination, and a separate and bounded self becomes the ideal. Reality seems to consist of surfaces, gestures, objects, scenes, and immediate perceptions rather than in structure, interpretation, or relation.[8]

If EPiC MAP can be invisibly efficient doing five things at once, "show, don't tell" is doing even more (I'm counting at least six simultaneous functions, if I err in the direction of granting that the craft advice is still as ubiquitous as it seems to me):

- it mistakes scene for narrative itself;
- it trains readers to equate immediacy with truth;
- it suppresses authorial intelligence by coding explicit statements as heavy-handed;

- it privileges private perception over collective, historical, or cosmological forms of meaning;
- it converts a classroom heuristic into institutional orthodoxy;
- and it makes an aesthetic of realism feel like common sense rather than history.[9]

What is most striking for me are the questions not about craft or literary criticism but questions about "soul-making" (in the broadest sense): how our attention is trained, how reality-feeling is formed, how certain habits of perception become authoritative, and how a person is shaped by the forms through which they imagine life. Stories do not just reflect experience; they train the ways experience is perceived. They teach reverence, denial, estrangement, kinship, mastery, porosity, or separation. This is all profoundly spiritual terrain even if the institutions involved are—or claim to be—secular.

Another rabbit hole in this chapter considers how aesthetic form and style create (or preclude) conditions for ethical, philosophical, or spiritual insight. Another enormous question, and another example: While pursuing an MFA in fiction at Arizona State University, I had a teacher with a tool kit of recurring rhetorical questions directed, when needed, at whichever student writer had a story being "workshopped" at the time. One of these questions for the aspiring author was: "What's the biggest coincidence that's ever happened to you?" It was meant to instruct the student away from using anything like a Dickensian coincidence as a plot device and to suggest that this student was perhaps leaning a little too close to using one in their pages. The student was not really supposed to respond but to silently admit that plot-resolving coincidences didn't happen to anyone. And we all got the message. Coincidence was being excluded not only as implausible plotting, but as an inadmissible theory of experience. Coincidences and synchronicities were not acceptable parameters of experience to steer with when writing American realist fiction, which is what everybody in that particular class was learning how to write.

When it comes to living a life, however, coincidences and synchronicities may indeed be legitimate parameters of experience to steer with. (What living a life as an American and writing American fiction have to do with each other is, I guess, a different kind of question.) Is reality really exhausted by secular rational causality, or is there meaningful pattern, synchronicity, providence, fate, grace, omen, or unseen relation with any kinds of claims on our lives? This is not just a narratological issue; it is a spiritual issue about what kinds of order or meaning may be present in the world and which among them modern realism trains us not to perceive.

It's been a long while since I've been in a workshop, or taught one, and I know there have been some profoundly creative and innovative new works about them, and for them, since I've "retired." For example, Melissa Febos, in *Body Work,* pushes back against inherited craft prohibitions by defending personal narrative as a serious mode of knowledge rather than a lesser, indulgent, or insufficiently disciplined form, thereby resisting older workshop suspicions of confession, intimacy, and overt self-implication. And Christopher Kempf, in *Craft Class,* treats the workshop not as a neutral training ground but as a historically specific American institution whose language of "craft" carries classed, professionalizing, and gatekeeping assumptions; and he works against precisely that institutional common sense. Significantly, Matthew Salesses, in *Craft in the Real World,* argues directly that what creative writing programs often present as universal craft principles are in fact culturally situated norms, and he explicitly rethinks workshop practice against those older institutionalized standards. As Salesses has argued, workshop "craft" rules such as "show, don't tell" are not universal but culturally situated norms: Yes! My concern is with tracing a longer literary genealogy for those norms and by asking what ontology of self and relation, and cosmovision, they naturalize. The arc is *long.*

In other words, workshops did not invent these assumptions—hardly. And some of the best writing teachers today, many of my close friends among them, are working hard at interrogating these assumptions. But workshops *are* one of the places where a local aesthetic became portable, teachable, and easy to enforce. One can point to a paragraph and call it "telling"; one can praise "scene work," "character depth," "psychological acuity," "earned motive," "immersion." Publishing may well reinforce the same preferences by rewarding prose that is quickly legible, image-rich, emotionally accessible, and often screen-adjacent. Reviewing refines them. Readers internalize them. John Gardner's famous formulation of fiction as a "vivid and continuous dream" belongs to this history too, even if *The Art of Fiction* is now an older craft text rather than a work of literary theory. What now feels like innocent taste is better understood as a historically produced competence in reading one particular aesthetic as if it were reality itself.[10]

Why does any of this matter, especially in a spiritually leaning book that claims not to be for academia? Stories, however they're told, reorganize perception more deeply than propositional information because they don't merely tell us something; they stage a world, distribute attention, assign salience, model causality, and allow us to inhabit patterns of feeling and judgment "from the inside." By contrast, consider scientific language: It is indispensable for many kinds of knowledge, but it usually does not by itself supply lived orientation. It can tell us that climate systems are collapsing, that extinction rates are accelerating, that inequality is widening. A story can make those facts legible as experience, motive, memory, conflict, obligation, loss. Stories are not stronger because they're "irrational." They're stronger because they operate at the level where value, identification, and reality-feeling are formed. And it's not that stories make us "more empathetic," though sometimes they do. Rather, it's that no society can do without forms that interpret experience, contest official reality, preserve memory, imagine alternatives, and examine the metaphors through which a culture understands personhood, nature, history, and obligation; as Martha Nussbaum has iterated in *Love's Knowledge and Poetic Justice,* this isn't supplementary to knowledge but part of it. I add to it, all of this, the importance and primacy of having a biologically living (and dying) body where all of this takes place.

Stories can entrench bad thinking as well as transform it. Narrative helps shape what a world is felt to be, and a narrative regime that privileges bounded individuals, plausible scenes, and inwardly sourced motive will predictably struggle to render distributed causality, ecological interdependence, and more-than-human agency as anything other than backdrop, pressure, symbol, or crisis. Climate catastrophe enters as weather, setting, or plot trigger, not as a challenge to the underlying metaphysics of personhood and world. Other beings—trees, rivers, animals, ancestors, atmospheres—appear as things encountered by a human subject, not as constitutive participants in a field of relation. Here, what might seem to be my mere literary complaint becomes something a little larger: In some cosmologies, relation is not secondary but fundamental; selfhood is conditional, porous, and constituted through reciprocity rather than sealed in advance. A craft system built on individuated being and derivative relation will not merely fail to represent such worlds well but will tend not to recognize them as real in the first place. This is one reason Amitav Ghosh's argument in *The Great Derangement* about the modern novel's difficulty with climate scale matters so much: The problem is not only thematic inadequacy but formal and ontological inadequacy.[11]

I hope it's clear that the issues I'm curious about here do not rely upon mainstream literary fiction lacking sophistication or workshop advice being "wrong." Rather, it is that one historically specific way of organizing reality came to feel like reality itself; and I was taught to call that not only craft but great writing, literature, and art. Often, it is all of these. My point is not to deny its power, but to notice its metaphysical assumptions before mistaking them for neutrality.

Finally, a last question: If it is true that we can only write what we know, how might we characterize our relationship with aesthetic forms that circumscribe not only what we do know but also *how* we can know it? This would mean that aesthetic forms are not simply containers for prior knowledge but help produce the horizons of intelligibility within which experience can be recognized, ordered, and rendered sayable. The issue is no longer only what a writer knows, but how form has already trained the writer's sense of what counts as knowledge, experience, or reality in the first place. If this is right, then formal experiment may be an attempt to know otherwise: to loosen the hold of inherited aesthetic arrangements and make room for experiences, relations, or realities that those arrangements have been unable to register. The question, then, is not only whether we can write beyond what we know, but also whether the forms available to us have already shaped the limits of knowing itself.

But never mind; this digression has gone on long enough. I don't want to foreground here conversations about mimesis and becoming, about how and whether literature's social or political role might diminish its aesthetic autonomy, whether aesthetic autonomy might undermine literature's ethical responsibilities (how can a literature have ethical responsibilities?), or how we're to read and consider any of this in the age of AI and identity politics. Those are, again, good topics for another day.

But for those of you who don't imagine teaching literature or creative writing comes with forbidding responsibility, think again. And for those of you who are writing students, or writers, or great readers, I will offer a single, clear-eyed view on these matters and move on. "If you find teachers who perpetuate your fears," says the author Perdita Finn, "leave them."[12]

I have felt all my ghosts leave me and now sense the ghosts leaving all of us.

In June 2019, my marriage ended and so did the predominant narrative of my life. This is, I suppose, not an uncommon thing to happen to adults in America, but mine, I think, was an extreme case. At my wife's urging I'd just accepted a new job out of state. We'd sold our house and were set to fly to Arkansas the next day to look at new ones. But now none of that would be happening: My wife wouldn't be moving to Arkansas with me and neither, she informed me, would our six-year-old son. In that moment, in the kitchen of the house that was no longer ours, as the green, leaf-filled light filtered through the window and landed on the yellow floor, I felt the story of my life, the story I'd been telling myself for thirty-seven years, end. It was a physical sensation that began in my throat and then a sudden drop. Then the only thing I knew for certain was what I no longer was.

Stories, I've since realized, are like ghosts. They haunt you, possess you, animate you, give spirit to the flesh. Over the course of my life, I've been visited by terrible stories. Stories that turned my life and the lives of those around me into grotesqueries, living nightmares. Cancer stories, stories of human cruelty, irrecoverable loss. I've been visited by benevolent and flattering ones as well.

That summer I was possessed by a series of stories that transformed me into a person I didn't recognize. I begged for my old job back. I applied for a job in Ohio that required a drug test and failed the test. I got into a shouting match so badly with my wife that a friend of hers called the cops. Who was I? In the absence of everything I knew for certain, who had I become?

Luckily none of those humiliating, angry, degrading narratives lingered long enough to do more than scare me deeply, but similarly none of the better stories I'd been possessed by had long-lasting effects. I told myself I'd become a Buddhist and meditate to fix my soul, because surely for this to happen to me, my soul must be broken. I told myself I'd find a job in Ohio so I wouldn't have to move to Arkansas and become a long-distance dad. It was mid-June and I was supposed to start my new job in August. I'd change my life completely in a month and a half. With the money from the house my wife and I sold, I bought a condo in Columbus to plant my flag.

But August came and I was still the person I had been at the beginning of summer: scared, confused, reeling. I was someone to whom things happened. I had no internal narrative, no sense of who I was supposed to be.

In college, for reasons both too complicated and banal to get into, I majored in German. Much of what I learned over the course of those four years has faded—my mastery of the grammar and vocabulary, the names of important figures, and specific dates—but one single word lodged itself in my memory from the moment I learned it: *entgeistert*. The closest literal translation is "disenchanted." Though in the context I encountered it, in the slim novella by Bodo Kirchhoff titled *Mexikanische Novelle*, the word means something closer to "post-haunted," or as my professor, the German novelist Gregor Hens, explained it: "a place where the ghosts have left."

In my twenties, I found the idea mysterious and romantic. What did it mean to be "post-haunted"? What was it like to live in some place that's been abandoned even by its *ghosts*? But at thirty-seven, in the throes of my divorce, I knew exactly what this meant. I had no guiding narrative. My ghosts had left me. I felt horrible, hollow, gray inside, like a house after all the furniture's been taken out.

I also appreciated the comedy: Of course there was a German word for that.

In August I listed my condo on Airbnb, loaded my car, said goodbye to my son, and drove to Arkansas to start a job that I'd once thought would launch a new "chapter" in my life but now felt meaningless. I rented a room, taught my classes, went for long bike rides, woke in the predawn hours from terrible dreams that always ended with my wife whispering my name in my ear, and drove back to Columbus every two weeks for the court-mandated time with my son. Months passed like that, though I honestly can't tell you anything that happened. If I wanted anything, it was to summon the ghosts that had left me, the stories that had once animated my now empty shell.

Then in March 2020 COVID struck, and it wasn't just my ghosts that fled. The world became *entgeistert*. The old stories no longer applied: stories about progress, about plans, about stability, about how next month would resemble the one that had just passed. For a while we thought they'd return—but they never did.

Work went remote and I moved back to the condo in Columbus. I ordered groceries online and sprayed them with bleach before I took them into the house. My son lived with me half the time. We baked bread, adopted guinea pigs. That summer when it was time to move back to Arkansas, I bought and restored a ruined house, its floors so rotted I kept stepping through.

For a while, the house gave me something like a story. Tasks. Lumber to replace. Nails to pull. Rot had edges. Damage had a place. Each day I knew what to fix. From the outside, this might have looked like stability. From the inside it felt more like noise. I told myself this was recovery. You fix what's in front of you and don't ask for more. And for long stretches of time, that story held. I worked. I answered emails. I paid bills. In the fall, my son lived with me for two weeks at a time while he attended classes online.

But the thing about that story is that it didn't last, either. Just like the stories that I tried to summon during the summer of my divorce, it arrived with force and then drained away, leaving the empty gray behind. It wasn't the wrong story. It was just a story, and stories didn't seem to stay.

I fixed the house and the routines thinned. The old blankness returned, not dramatic, not even sad, just vacant—a hollow feeling in the back of my throat.

By then the rest of the world had begun reckoning with its own long aftermath. The pandemic didn't end so much as dissolved into everything. Politics grew simultaneously abstract and feral. Each year felt less like a new chapter and more like a continuation of a long and unwinding scroll—events accumulating without making any sense.

The ghosts didn't just leave me; they've left the premises. The big stories that once structured time have dimmed into the background. The bulb is still warm but no longer lit.

Sometimes, early in the morning I walk my dog before the sun comes up. The neighborhood is silent in that padded, prehuman way. Dark houses. No voices. No cars.

And sometimes, without warning, a thought arrives with the same physical certainty I felt in my throat the day my marriage ended.

I want to go home.

The thought is so clear it feels like a memory. But standing there on the sidewalk, leash in hand, I can't for the life of me picture where that home might be. I only know that, wherever it is, the ghosts aren't there anymore. What I'm really missing is that old feeling of being haunted.

—Bryan Hurt, writer and miracle-maker, Cleveland, OH

–6–

No Analysis

The challenge is not to interpret at all—certainly not in the moment—to hold an experience that can feel between language, that can leave one with tension of holding one's intellectual and rational breath for far longer than any of us can imagine doing. To not seek the comfort of rational understanding, but to come to some kind of knowing through a holding and a wonderment.

—JEROME BERNSTEIN, *Living in the Borderland*

At the ancient pond
a frog plunges into
the sound of water

—BASHO (translated by Sam Hamill), *The Sound of Water*

EXPLANATION HAS ITS PLACE, but it can't replace lived experience. My objection here is not to thought but to thought that arrives too early—especially where it is seeking solutions to conditions not yet fully experienced—or where it claims too much. Jerome Bernstein's words describe how these days I make sense of Daishin's *Don't tell stories.* Daishin himself might have put it this way: First, experience the question *Who am I?* without any conceptual scaffolding or gutter bumpers and instead with your *whole body.* "Live your questions now," writes Rainer Maria Rilke. Afterward, perhaps later, a useful or helpful story about that experience will emerge that you can share. But don't force a story. And certainly don't force it or tell it while you're in the midst of trying to experience something, such as sushi, hot sake, and good company.

And there was nothing in the world like Daishin's company at a meal. The first time I was to join him for lunch, I was so nervous—meeting a Zen teacher for lunch! Did I know all the rules? What to eat, what not to eat, how to eat, when to eat . . .? We met at Papa Cristo's, which is right around the corner from Zen Center of Los Angeles, and where you line up, make your order at the counter, then take a number and find a seat. I'm not sure if I finagled for him to be ahead of me in line just to watch and be sure to match my choices somehow to his (for far too long, I was *that* kind of student), but he was ahead of me in line, and when it was his turn to order, he smiled at the cashier and said, "I'll take the lamb kebabs and the biggest damn beer you've got!"

"Aim for a negative capability," he once told me, loving John Keats and all poetry, as he did. For Keats, this is the capacity for "being in uncertainties, Mysteries, doubts, without any irritable reaching after fact and reason"[1] and is the very heart of what Zen folk call "not-knowing" (not to be mistaken, Eve Marko once reminded me, with actual ignorance). And this is important to add. Because even once I did report an experience, or tell a story as it were, I had to be careful not to get ambitious in interpreting as I shared, not to work in some elaborate theory explaining what had occurred. This could be funny; I remember once, after a sitting period, feeling wise and magnanimous and sharing out loud something I thought I'd understood about the practice, to which Daishin said, "Talking to yourself again, eh?" But it could be serious, too. On one occasion, working my way one step forward, two steps back through a long episode of clinical depression, I met with Daishin face-to-face for a teacher-student interview, and through tears and in suicidal despair told him I was "trapped in my body." At that moment, in that half hour, Daishin was tender and warm but no less clear that this, too, was an interpretation I was adding on top of my grief.

Being neck-deep in words and text all day, every day, didn't make it easier, but originally I never did have my sights set on "being a writer"—a storyteller of that kind. Yes, I had willfully majored in English as an undergrad (this was less goal-driven than rooted in the then American belief that I could and should simply study what I "liked"), but it had been a set of fairly arbitrary circumstances that led me to pursue a graduate degree in writing. My life a couple of autumns after college was falling apart in one of those common, young-adult ways of that age: I was writing for a newspaper, which was wonderfully instructive work, but it was in a small town, the one my college boyfriend was from and where we were living together—until we weren't. I believed I had no prospects, did not want to move back home with my parents, and needed a plan that involved moving far away. There was no time to study for the LSAT or to write anything really incisive, but, though I had never taken a creative writing class, I thought I could draft the beginning of a novel filled with provocative and daring narrative threads I would never have to resolve, as I only needed to send in the first thirty pages. Beginning an MFA would at least give me somewhere to go and something to do in the immediate term while I figured out a real plan. Curiously, I recall more clearly than this intentionally incomplete draft the personal statement that accompanied it.

Probably because of so much reading up to that point, I had developed what I can only describe as a kind of internalized narrative stutter—and this was the subject of that personal statement. When looking out at the Bitterroot Mountains of northern Idaho after graduating college, I'd think, *I was looking out at the Bitterroot Mountains of northern Idaho* . . . or worse, She *was looking out* . . . Couldn't I just stand there, looking at (I was far from being able to "join" or "communicate with") the mountain without all of this chatter? Did I really believe my actual life was being or needed to be recorded for a diligent reader who was entirely a figment of my own imagination? I felt like my enormous student loans had been taken out to buy a mental illness. (I feel even more so now. And just by the way, as of today, more than twenty-five years later, I am still paying off those undergraduate loans. I am in good standing. Aside from deferral while I was in graduate school, I have never paused in the monthly payments.)

So this internal narrator of mine was far too noisy, and somehow, I reflected in that application essay, an MFA might teach me how to make it stop. Maybe I just needed to sort of get it off my chest by writing a book. The main problem an MFA was going to solve was not that I needed to learn to write; the problem I wanted it to address (in addition to needing somewhere to go) was that in a decade and a half of school, I'd constructed a self that was modeled on and out of text, almost exclusively (and certainly by concepts where it wasn't actual text). And not just any text, but text in *English*. Which I had *majored in*. Deconstructing a self and dropping the bully of the worldview that dictated its experiences, if I could and to the extent that it seemed useful or important to do so—that was the task at hand.

And so it remains—because it is a lifetime practice, dropping conceptual constructions to enter fully into lived experience. In her foreword on finding the kind of stories that we might need today, Jane Hirshfield writes, "Sometimes a person needs to think in ways beyond linear logic, to think by feeling, by leap, by empathy's emptying us of all concept of self and other."

And to this she adds that we are not alone, for many someones have left trails of breadcrumbs behind them. Here are some: Dogen Zenji says, "To study the self is to forget the self. To forget the self is to be actualized by myriad things."[2] Drop the stories—drop all those conceptual constructions—and see what's left. "The person is merely the result of a misunderstanding," writes Nisargadatta Maharaj. "In reality, there is no such thing."[3]

This isn't something to be afraid of. The lesson of impermanence can be exhilarating, liberating, and a huge relief. The poet and my dear old friend Henry Oso Quintero put it this way in conversation recently:

> A really uncolonized way of encountering story is to *be* the story. If you can be patient with the story and what it's offering you, you understand your impermanence in life. This is so important a thing it transcends all schools of spirituality. We get hung up on Buddhism. Peyote as a Native American churchism. The Apache Way. The Comanche Way. Whether it's Kazu, whether it's Zen, then what kind of Zen it is . . . Fucking A! They are *all so wonderful*!

When I asked him to give me an example of understanding impermanence by way of being a story, Henry told me about some of the ceremony in and by and with which he has been raised: "When I sing The Last Song, I'm not singing The Last Song. That makes it sound like it's a possession. The song sings me. I *become* the eight-year-old boy who originally sang that song. When I sing it, I *am* that boy." He shared with me a story of an outsider once coming to the fire and hearing the song sing Henry; this was a person who subsequently laughed at how high and small the wonderfully large Henry's voice had been while singing. "He didn't understand it," Henry said, "that there was no Henry while the boy's song sang me."

If my path from that first writing degree to a zendo was tortured (so many blessings of humiliation on that road), I did get there eventually and not *too* much later. But it didn't have to be a zendo. There are as many ways to fully enter into one's lived experience and empty one's self of the concept of self and other as there are ways to spend a minute of your life: chopping onions, walking, cleaning dishes, shoveling mulch, riding a bicycle, climbing a mountain, hauling trash. If it's simple, and it is, it is the next step that can get really dicey—the aforementioned step where we can stop and interpret everything that's going on and come up with a really great theory to explain it, or instead, accept the experience and carry on. Beyond suggesting some resonance with relational cosmovisions and pushing up against the limits of a one-world cosmovision, there isn't a contribution in this book that is meant to serve as the ground of a new theory of anything. They are not meant to be leveraged as tools for or against this theory or that. Tiokasin Ghosthorse once shared with me that among the Lakota there is a saying that if you stop counting the stars, you will die. The number of stars is incalculable; it is a mystery. If you ever think, *I've done it, I've got it, done . . .* you are, again, mountains and rivers away. Take your seat again, you who believe you have attained enlightenment, and go back to zero.

Here's a wonderful example, in my view, of an experience shared story-wise without interpretation. Early last summer I was in the Arizona mountains with my children. We were out at night, every night, walking and looking up at the bright crush of stars, listening to the javelina skirt around in the near distance and remarking on what were to them wholly new fragrances of desert flora. After one of those evening walks, one of my children said, "The strangest thing happens when you really look at the stars."

"Tell me about it," I said.

"First you feel like all of a sudden you have no idea what they are. Then you realize you never did know what they are."

"Ha. That's right."

"But at the same time, they are so weirdly familiar, like of course you have known them forever because you are basically them."

We were all quiet for several seconds.

"What does that feel like?" I asked. "That kind of experience?"

"It feels like an amazing miracle, then it's over. Though you still feel kind of curious about it. Like, what was *that*?"

It was the almost perfect formulation of an encounter or experience in the world that happens quickly, unsummoned amid attention and openness, and that, though over in a flash, leaves just a little residue of curiosity. It is this residue of curiosity that one of my Zen teachers, Roshi Susan Myoyu Andersen, equated with faith. Faith is not, she shared with us, an abstract concept. It is more like when you're reaching behind the couch cushions, way deep into the couch, to grab a pen. You know it's there because your fingertips just brushed the end of it, but you can't grab it; or you know it's there because a moment ago, you had it in your hand.

The strangest thing happens when you really look at the stars in the desert. First you feel like all of a sudden you have no idea what they are. Then you realize you never did know. But at the same time, they are so weirdly familiar like of course you have known them forever because you basically are them. It feels like an amazing miracle, then it's over. Though you still feel kind of curious. Like, what was *that*?

HE DIDN'T GET CAUGHT UP in interpreting his own experience. Being a child was surely in his favor in this regard.

In the Zen liturgy, there is an apt line in a poem called "Song of the Jewel Mirror Awareness" by Master Dongshan Liangjie and which describes the nondual, ever-present nature of "reality." The line in question goes, "Turning away and touching are both wrong, for it is like a massive fire."[4] I think of this so often—it is a good and simple formula to keep handy in the world, in relation to some experiences, such as envy or lust or insight or winning an award. It's saying, *Don't make a big thing out of it, but don't ignore it either.* It's saying, *Don't try to grasp this thing, don't believe it, but don't dismiss it.* It's sort of like the saying "It's not nothing."

What does it feel like to experience being the stars? It feels like an amazing miracle, then it's over; though you still feel kind of curious about it, like what was *that*?

Here's another, again from my friend Tiokasin.

In 2019, I spent some time in Cyprus. At dinner time, a giant blue Egyptian scarab flew onto my shoulder. I was at peace. I don't know what that means, but it was something different.

—Tiokasin Ghosthorse, educator and musician of the Cheyenne River Lakota, SD

IT ISN'T ALWAYS, OR EVER, EASY—this commitment to full body awareness and direct experience without analysis. (And of course there are many situations in which analysis is the imminent task at hand—it may be literally your job.) Especially not if you've been conditioned to believe that being smart is a particularly valuable thing or that any and every legitimate experience has a rational explanation.

In his 1620 work *Novum Organum,* Francis Bacon writes, "The human understanding when it has once adopted an opinion . . . draws all things else to support and agree with it."[5] Noted: Resist layering interpretation on top of observation, especially if my thinking tends to bend toward certain preexisting ideas about the world and its mysteries. It can be astonishingly difficult not to interpret and try to make sense of a mysterious experience. See if you can catch where, in reading the story below, your thinking brain might be engaging in an attempt to explain it all to yourself, or for Laura van den Berg, who doesn't need an explanation and beautifully accepts the gift and keeps the spoken words to herself.

The night after my father died, I had an overwhelmingly vivid dream that he was speaking to me through my sister's dog, a brown-and-white pit bull named Champ. Then I woke up in my sister's guest room in Florida, in the middle of the night, and her dog was sitting upright on the bed and staring down at me, his jaws opening and closing as though controlled by a ventriloquist's strings. He was speaking, I could just barely hear the words. It was an amazing encounter that I felt deeply and will never fully understand.

—Laura van den Berg, novelist, Winter Park, FL

SOMETIMES THESE EXPERIENCES are so nuanced and complex, it doesn't matter if we *do* try to interpret them—they resist it; they are foolproof, as it were. These are experiences we can examine for years, from this lens and that lens, and nothing will yield itself up but deeper mystery. The Tao that can be told is not the Tao. So it has been for Egyoku regarding a significant vision she once had.

In 1983, the Zen center was in terrible upheaval over the conduct of its founding abbot. During that time, I was serving as *jishin*, the attendant to the founders. Every day, three times a day at dawn, noon, and twilight, I would go to the Founders Room and perform the appropriate rituals. After several years of serving in this way, I was deeply immersed in the energies of the room. Our founding abbot left the Zen center to enter alcohol rehabilitation, and the sangha was in turmoil. One day I had a vision in broad daylight: I saw a huge bald eagle standing at the bowing mat in front of the founders' altar, clothed in a golden robe, its wings spread wide. The eagle stood from floor to ceiling; its outstretched wings, spread from wall to wall, protected the entire altar. Then my gaze focused on the right foot of the eagle, where a tiny sparrow was sheltering. I saw this scene with startling clarity. For years afterward, I spoke to no one about it and wondered what it might mean. About five years later, I attended the Harmonia Mundi peace conference. My teacher, the abbot, and his attendant were also taking part. We participated in a workshop together; the abbot and attendant were paired for an exercise. While I don't recall the particulars of the exercise, nor of my own experiences, it had to do with each participant becoming an animal. After it was over, the attendant and I met outside of the room. "That was something," he said to me, a bit bewildered.

"Oh really," I replied. "What animal were you?"

"I was an eagle," he said.

"And what was Roshi (the abbot)?" I asked.

The attendant said, "He was a sparrow."

Then I told him about my vision all those years ago. He was floored. I was, too. Still today I ponder the meaning of this.

—Wendy Egyoku Nakao, Zen Center of Los Angeles abbot emeritus, Honolulu, HI

IN A WAY, CATHOLIC SCHOOL—which I loved for many reasons, for the mysteries and the liturgy and perhaps especially for the organ music that sounded like wind playing upon hollow bones—it primed me for such a practice. There was a rule in some of the classrooms at St. Ann's that when you finished your assigned work, you'd clear off your desk, fold your hands before you, sit perfectly still, and meditate on the cross. There was a crucifix in every room. Thus you'd wait, eyes fixed on a dead or dying Christ, for everyone else to finish their work, too. Being a quick worker, I spent hours—hours and hours—of my childhood in this position, considering what it was to die, nailed to a cross, swinging across a chasm of wonder and terror, faith and doubt. The direction was to sit at your desk and, though there was no real instruction beyond that, to silently contemplate the cross. To pay it great and reverential attention. To know it was sacred and beyond your understanding. This was an "assignment" that would never end and an answer you would never reach, because the question wasn't a question—it was something you were supposed to *do*.

When they're not crowded out by our ingenious theories, the kinds of fleeting insights described by contributors in this chapter—they're the kinds of experiences that can make a person wonder how much else there is out there that remains invisible and unknown. Once, I was cleaning the Zen Center of Los Angeles kitchen with Gary Koan Janka, one of our teachers, and we discovered a portion of the countertop was on wheels, so we wheeled it out of place and were able to scrub away a good deal of collected dust, paperclips, pencil ends, shriveled carrot tops, and other forgotten scraps. I was feeling so satisfied. "Doesn't that make you feel good?" I asked Koan Sensei. "No," he said, eyes sparkling. "It makes me wonder how much more I'm missing."

–7–

Ordinary Relationship

Isolated material particles are abstractions;
their properties are definable and observable only through
their interaction with other systems.

—NIELS BOHR, "Discussion with Einstein on
Epistemological Problems in Atomic Physics"

We are the embodiment of each other's struggles.

—JUNE JORDAN, "Report from the Bahamas, 1982"

I used to have a dog, Eleanor, with whom I would spend a lot of time trail running. There was a big park near where we lived with miles and miles of single-track trails on either side of a creek. I could let her run off leash alongside me, free to pause to sniff whatever smells, and then sprint to catch up or bound ahead. While most of the park was wild, there was a busier area in the center with a stone bridge across the creek and little restaurant. It was a picturesque spot that attracted well-dressed crowds for brunch or weddings or whatnot.

One day, Eleanor and I were coming into this area at the end of a long run. I would have been sweaty, and both of us would have been dirty—a stark contrast with the brunch and photo crowd. At the end of the creek, there was a Canada goose with a cluster of little goslings, still young enough to be bright yellow. With a reaction time that surpassed my human perceptual skills, Eleanor, a retriever mix, took off after them without a thought. It's striking to see instinct at work. She was fast, and these geese were not prepared for anything more threatening than well-dressed toddlers. In an instant, she had one of the goslings in her mouth. I was horrified, both for the gosling and for the scene that we were creating for the onlookers.

But as soon as she had the gosling in her mouth, she completely shifted. She stopped and looked at me, seemingly confused. It was as though instinct had shut off. And with thought returned, she seemed to be aware that this was not a ball or a stick but an animate life in her mouth. *What am I supposed to do?* her look seemed to be asking me. *This is alive.* In that moment, I felt like I was directly seeing another mind suddenly confronted with the shocking awareness of another life.

I was able to run over to her, ease open her jaws, and the still-alive gosling dropped into the water. It immediately dove underwater and swam furiously out into the creek. A few seconds later, it popped up behind its siblings in an orderly line behind the adult, out in the middle of the creek, to which they had quickly retreated.

—Nicolas Cornell, professor of law, Brunswick, ME

OF COURSE A DOG wants to chase a gosling, and I recently had a similar experience with a rescue puppy and duckling. The duckling didn't make it, though the puppy was not looking for a meal and did not know what to make of the small bird he had crushed. What is so amazing to me about Nico's story is the strength of relationship he shared with Eleanor. It was such that Eleanor herself, realizing there was something different about the sensation of taking a living creature into her mouth, looked to her human companion in confusion, in question, in shock. The truth is, the duckling my own puppy crushed in his jaws died in my hands, and it was terrible; I wish the pup had known his name, had known me, had had any training in him at all that would've allowed for a different outcome. When I talked with Nico about this story, it was the weirdness of the entire scene that seemed so improbable to him. I'm sure had Eleanor intentionally or accidentally killed the gosling, Nico would have managed the situation as gracefully as he could and would have found sympathy in the brunch crowd. But that's not what happened. I love this story most for the moment Eleanor pauses and looks to Nico—for the moment when their eyes meet. The very recognition seems to assume a life of its own.

Once as a hospital chaplain, I visited with a patient who was—as so many of us are—one paycheck away from poverty. She was a CNA who suddenly began having unexplainable medical episodes and so could no longer work with the elderly clientele that her job entailed. In that same season, amid seeking medical help, she lost her apartment and began living out of her car. It was not clear when her surgical procedure was over whether or where she would have shelter or for how long. But I visited her three times during that hospital stay, and during one visit she told me the following story.

So I was living out of my car and feeling pretty lonely and scared at night because I was a woman alone—and let me say again, alone. Because when you don't have another person or a dog or someone with you, there's not much God around either. It can feel like that. Abandoned. So this one night I was really hungry. I was often hungry, but sometimes it just hits you harder, and what I really wanted was fried chicken. I wanted a whole pan of it at home in my mom's kitchen. I wanted it so bad I was crying, and I drove over to where the fast-food restaurants were, because one of them was a Popeyes, and I parked on the street in front of it and felt sorry for myself. Then I started to pray, not for Taco Bell or a chicken sandwich but for God to please just put someone else in my life for a minute. If the hunger wouldn't kill me, the loneliness would. So I have my head down on the steering wheel, eyes closed, had that kind of tiredness that comes after a long cry. And someone taps on my door. I startled, and it was a teenager looking me right in the eye through the window. I turned on the car and rolled it down a little and he lifted a plastic bag. It was a box of chicken. "I don't know if you need it or want it," he said. But they were about to close and he saw me out there, so he brought it over. When I think of this story, before I think of the chicken, I think of that moment looking that kid in the eye. That was God's eye.

—Anonymous, Rochester, MN

"MAY WE FIND MOMENTS OF ENCOUNTER EVEN IN ISOLATION," the Irish poet Pádraig Ó Tuama writes.[1] This kind of compassion and significance that arises in open, attentive connection between people is something I have experienced many times as a hospital chaplain: If I enter the room open, and open to connection, connecting happens. And not just any connection; there is a spirit in, or of, that connection that is neither me, nor the patient. We both feel it. Often the patient themselves will remark on its quality; sometimes they will mistakenly attribute it to me, but it is definitely not me. I say precious little in a patient encounter, especially in the first ten or fifteen minutes. Rather, I am attempting to stay present and grounded (*Where are your feet?* Joan Halifax's words echo in my head)—an apparently simple task that can be quite complicated by some of the circumstances a person encounters in emergency rooms, trauma burn units, pediatric oncology. "We cannot realize [anything] without the presence of relatedness," says Joan Halifax. "This is where spirit appears—not in an individual but between individuals. When this happens, the distinction between self and other simply vanishes."[2]

Again and again this kind of numinous interconnection with another person has brought to mind Matthew 18:20: "For where two or three are gathered together in my name, there am I in the midst of them." There are variations of these sacred words across traditions. Among the Lakota, it is expressed that when people gather with good hearts, right intention, and respect, the sacred is present. The prophet Muhammad said, "No people gather to remember Allah except that tranquility (*sakinah*) descends upon them, mercy envelops them, the angels surround them, and Allah mentions them among those who are with Him." From Pirkei Avot 3:2, "Two who sit together and have no words of Torah between them—this is a gathering of scoffers . . . But two who sit together and words of Torah are between them—the Shekhinah [or presence of God] rests between them."

And while I appreciate this may be controversial for some readers, I will note here, and add more in the pages ahead, that in beginning work exploring animal chaplaincy, scripture and teachings such as these hold as powerfully and beautifully true in a group of human and nonhuman animals gathered together as they do in a hospital room or classroom of humans alone. Part of what is so beautiful and important about the story below is that it is indeed a story—not the contributor's, Lana's, direct experience; she has told me how much this story of her grandmother and the cow has lived in and shaped her. The stories we tell have lives of their own.

My grandmother was orphaned in Belarus at the age of fifteen; the eldest of ten children, she found herself suddenly in loco parentis. This was around the time of the 1917 revolutions. Within a year she married and had to make heartbreaking decisions about the care of her siblings. She placed some in orphanages and was able to care for some with her new husband. Despite the family farm, they could barely afford shoes. She and my grandfather decided to pack up everything, sell the farm and a small mill—sell everything and leave Belarus to pursue potential opportunities to work in Russia. As part of this, my grandmother (Vera, which means "faith" in Belarusian) had to sell her beloved cow, which she did.

The cow was sent off with her new owner, and the very next day Vera was due to leave by train for Russia. At the train station that day, she was astonished to encounter . . . her beautiful cow! She had come looking for Vera, and had found her, and they had a most tearful farewell there at the station. How did the cow know? How was she found? Questions that filled me with wonder.

My grandmother passed away many years ago now. I never doubted the truth of the story or the sensitivity and intelligence of the cow. One day, when my cat lifted her paw to wipe a silent tear from my cheek (true!), I was speechless and recalled my Babushka Vera's cow.

—Lana Nadj, lawyer, Kelowna, BC, Canada

SINCE I CAN'T INCLUDE PHOTOGRAPHS of this next story, I want you to imagine it: A man and a woman walking down a gravel road with two cats walking steadily alongside, all spread out with equal distance between each of them, and each with their intelligent face lifted upward to the morning. A family of four out to greet the day. Herding cats indeed! What else but meaningful relationship—and the trust, companionship, and love it entails—could hold them all together that way on every walk?

Every morning we take our cats Yale and Stanford out for a walk—no leashes.

—Valerie and Barry McCarthy, Oklahoma City, OK, and San Francisco, CA

ESTABLISHING—or rather opening to—real connection with another can be bungled. Half-baked. Taken for ordinary. But it is the kind of intimacy that can be cultivated precisely, as Jane Hirshfield says, by empathy's emptying the concept of self and other, and by acknowledging it where it happens. For every deeply relational story that's been shared with me over the past several months that "takes the top of my head off," as Emily Dickinson puts it of a good poem, there's another that seems on the surface rather familiar (at least to the extent that so many of us have such stories), reflecting just how easy it is to mistake that they are commonplace for a belief that they are unworthy of our attention or retelling.

One morning I headed to Lanikai Beach with my snorkel and fins, feeling low, like walls were closing in on me. I asked the universe to show me abundance. I got into an area of the ocean where I did not expect to see much. The sun was barely rising, so I'd barely be able to see through the layers of water into the coral reef. But just as I went under, in that very moment, right away, a multiplicity of newborn baby fish delighted me with their presence. As I thought to surface and turn to the shore, a big turtle soared up to greet me.

—*Gemma Cubero del Barrio, documentary filmmaker, Segovia, Spain*

When I was thirteen, my mother, three siblings, and I were sitting inside a rented car in a shady parking lot outside of a shabby Motel 6. We were in Georgia visiting a loved one in prison, but our original housing plans fell through, so we were driving around to different motels to see if they had any rooms left. We didn't have enough money to stay in a hotel at the time, nor, for that matter, did we have enough to stay in the Motel 6. All we needed was $200 to stay somewhere, but because we didn't have it, we were readying ourselves to spend a night or two in our car. In a moment of desperation (and quite honestly, exasperation), my siblings and I started praying to "Rah, Jah, God, Jesus, Confucius, and Allah" in the hopes that some sort of a miracle would happen. Though our pleas were somewhat uttered in jest (as cynical adolescents are wont to do), they were sincere. After that, we waited for our mom, who was still in the Motel 6 figuring things out. After a few minutes of waiting, my mother returned to the car jubilant while waving key cards. She informed us that while she was waiting in the lobby, during just that window, $200 magically appeared in her account—the exact amount that she needed to reserve a room for us. When she relayed the news, we screamed and cheered. We told her about our prayer, and she hugged and high-fived all four of us. That moment, and others like it, remind me that during the times when we feel like there is no relief in sight, someone/being/consciousness has us in theirs—and they might even give us a wink from time to time if we keep our eyes open. An old friend once told me during a difficult moment that "some call it God; I call it beauty." In that same vein, some call it a miracle, I call it a wink. Seeing my mother brimming with joy and relief that day was God winking. And, I might add, her eyes are works of beauty.

—Lla Anderson, Harvard University Divinity and Law School student, Fort Lauderdale, FL

I was newly separated from my spouse and taking care of my four minor children alone, with another in college. This was about one year after we'd had to sell our big house in North Carolina and move into a very small rental house in Nashville. My spouse became unemployed shortly after our separation, and my income as a musician was paltry and unreliable. I had no idea how I would make our rent payments, which were $2,050 per month. I knew that if I asked, my parents would give or loan me what I needed, and as the due date approached, I kept reaching for my phone to text them. But something kept me from doing it. I kept hearing, *Don't ask. Just wait. Just wait.*

About five days before rent was due, I received a message from a friend, saying he and his wife had just received an unexpected tax refund (this was in the early autumn, months later than most tax refunds are issued). He knew about our separation and my husband's unemployment but didn't have specifics about our finances or my rent worry. He said they wanted to gift the refund to me and suggested three separate installments over three months. The amount of each check they sent was $2,000, just what I needed to make my rent payments through the fall.

—Christa Wells, songwriter, Palo Pinto, TX

When I was struck by realization, it was as if Yukon had burst out laughing—an uncontained belly laugh, so much richer and far rarer than the carbonated good cheer of his everyday demeanor. Though he passed away on February 28, 2024, it was May of that year that he clearly, gleefully exclaimed, "Bosui, that took you long enough! Do you see, do you see now? What fun! I love you, Bose. I'm here!" I had been sitting in my mother's apartment, a day's journey from my home. It was early, and I sat cross-legged on a chair, sipping coffee and letting myself experience the deep, tight, contorted sensations that still came on unawares, an intense grief at the loss of this very special man in my life. It was then that, suddenly—urgently—a thought came: *What day was that that I was driving* (in an unfamiliar town, disoriented and a bit confused around how to get to my destination)*, when I looked up and saw the street sign that read "Yukon Street"?!* I reached for my phone, scrolled back through the photos, remembering how perfect it is that, having lost my way, I'd found myself on Yukon Street. I am no stranger to "signs," yet I feel next-level joy and awe (and not an ounce of surprise) that Yukon sent me (as of course he would!) a literal sign. "You're so intense, Bosui," he used to say, animated by glee. And I always heard, "Aw, sweetheart. Perhaps you'll outgrow that?"

I love you, Bose. I love you so much. I found the picture, grateful for the time stamp: April 16th. Just laying eyes on it, I felt a flash of the sweetness, but on its heels was another pressing, urgent probe. How many days after his death was this? Feeling urgent, I switched to the calendar app, counted the days. I counted a second time; then a third. Forty-nine days. Can that be real? Yukon sent me the literal sign forty-nine days after he'd passed!? I felt swirly with disorientation; and a growing heaviness—a skepticism. An it-can't-be-ness. I felt afraid and hopeful. So, what to do but turn to Google?

"In Buddhism, forty-nine days symbolizes the time between a person's death and their rebirth, a period often called the bardo or intermediate state. . . . This forty-nine-day period is also seen as a crucial time for grieving, with rituals helping the living to process their loss while also providing spiritual support for the deceased."

— *Max[ine] Christopher, interfaith spiritual care provider, Kansas City, MO*

My mother died peacefully at the age of ninety-three, the day after Christmas, on the nursing home unit of the retirement center where she had lived independently in a small apartment for three years. The day after, I returned to the center to begin emptying her apartment. All week I had been listening to the Seriously Sinatra station on the radio, knowing her time was coming. Listening to that music brought me smiles, thinking about the long, loving marriage my parents had together. They loved the music of the '40s and absolutely loved dancing together. For decades they danced. So I pulled into the parking lot, with the radio still on. I looked up and said out loud, "Oh, Mama, you're not here with me anymore." At that instant, Billie Holiday's version of "Cheek to Cheek" started: "Heaven, I'm in Heaven . . ."

That afternoon, I went to the church to arrange Mom's Mass. I had not been to this church since my father had passed away, twelve years prior. I pulled into the parking lot, at which time Mel Tormé's recording of "Cheek to Cheek" began. All I said was, "Okay, Dad, you're together now."

And yes—one more time. My daughters came into town for Mom's funeral. One afternoon, we all distracted ourselves a bit and went shopping. We walked into one of our favorite stores—and there was Billie Holiday again, singing "Cheek to Cheek." I just couldn't believe it.

—Deborah Melnyk, nurse (retired), Cleveland, OH

WHAT ARE THESE BUT COINCIDENCES, you might ask, or interesting but ordinary circumstances facilitated by another person? Indeed, that is what they are. And *another* person—Maxine, Christa, or Deborah, or Gemma, or Lla—might respond: And what is a coincidence but a remarkable occurrence with no rationally explainable causal connection that you can, if you wish, nevertheless explain away? As the physician Robert Lanza writes, "Mystery is never disproof."[3]

Still, the disagreement here comes from some of the differences across how we understand causation, probability, and meaning. Often such events are interpreted subjectively, especially when emotions are running high. We may seek meaning or patterns where none exist. Or we want to believe that the universe is purposeful (amid a culture that attempts to maintain as neutral the narrative that it is *not*). Similarly, sometimes we want to believe that God, or something or someone like God, is behind lifesaving "coincidences." We see synchronicity, providence, karma, or randomness in such events. Sometimes, when such occurrences happen in our own lives, they *do* take on meaning we may not have appreciated when hearing of others' similar tales; this is interesting and not unexpected given some of the reasons we are skeptical about coincidences. And it could be due to the people involved in our own similar experiences, or something else about the circumstances. I neither have nor offer any solution except for the guidance from my own teachers to meet these moments as they are, without attempting to explain them or explain them away, and to ride out the emotions that arise in response. The truth is, nobody knows. I recall when coteaching a class on death and dying at Carleton College, during a day we were talking about what comes after death, how many students stated firmly that they had no beliefs: After death, they said, there was nothing. That, I told them, is profound belief. The truth is, nobody knows.

In *Living in the Borderland*, the Jungian analyst Jerome Bernstein writes of a patient—an intelligent, psychologically functional young woman—who expressed distress regarding her experience of overwhelming physical and emotional pain whenever she passed by a feedlot or slaughterhouse. She did not, she said, merely empathize with the cows—she was fiercely adamant about this. Rather, she felt their suffering occurring inside her own body. Initially, in line with his extensive training, Bernstein looked to explain this experience through the patient's childhood trauma, attributing it to dissociation, projection, pathological overidentification, and symbolic displacement of her own suffering. But she continued to explain that her experience was visceral, immediate, and unbidden. She did not exhibit any signs of psychosis. Furthermore, she was self-aware and questioned the experience rather than believing it was "normal"; the phenomenon occurred only in specific environmental contexts (near cows destined for slaughter); and it had no metaphorical link to her personal history. Ultimately Bernstein recognized he was reacting as a Western-trained ego, trying to force her experience into a conceptual system that could not contain or explain it. He had to confront some uncomfortable questions: What if the patient's experience was not a projection but a form of nonordinary perception? What if reality is not as separate as Western rationalism assumes? He goes on to examine in *Living in the Borderland* a psychological and cultural space where the boundaries between the Western ego and the "other"—including nature and consciousness—grow permeable. As such, his work explores trauma, healing, ecological crisis, and the limits of Western rationalism. He proposes that psychological wholeness requires integrating ways of knowing traditionally excluded by Western thought.[4]

How much might our bodies, existing only in relationship with everything else mutually co-arising, be responding to the bodies of those around us in ways that we are conditioned not to notice or feel? What if we did notice and feel them? We might be grateful for the limits of our own awareness, for the seemingly temporary nature of its flashes of somatic empathy. If we could feel the effects of our actions in the world in relation to every other living body whom we otherwise understand to be property, or a food source, or as subordinate to humans (including other humans), life would be painful indeed. Then again, perhaps we *are* feeling the effects of these actions and this mindset. Perhaps that is precisely what modern life is like. By such a light, *treat others as you'd treat yourself* feels cautionary and ripe with information some of us are refusing or are no longer capable of seeing. As Matthew 25:40 expresses it, "Truly I tell *you*, whatever *you* did for one of the *least* of these brothers and sisters of mine, *you* did for *me*."

In any case, if we recognize or experience a more relational world view, we are in relationship not only with every*one* but also with every*thing*. All that appears ordinary may be far more mysterious than we walk around acknowledging. Experiencing ordinary moments as numinous is not reserved for specialists, mystics, or artists. Nothing in any of this book's contributions requires prestige to be a real thing.

I attended an office retreat some years ago just after completing a long silent Zen retreat and was asked the question in an ice-breaking group activity: "Tell us about one of the most mysterious and wonderful things that has happened to you." I tried in vain to quickly describe the experience of a day previous when I found myself drinking a cup of tea. I had stilled myself so thoroughly in an empty and dimly lit room that when suddenly there was a teacup before me, filled with fragrant water I could take into my body with a pleasing effect—I was astonished. To me, at the time and even a day later, it had seemed like the most impossible miracle. By now, that magic has faded, and that's a very good thing, or I would probably be focused on continually churning up the memory of it rather than focusing on whatever miracles might be arising now, in real time. And churning up and repeating a memory is a lot like what Daishin would call talking to yourself.

So perhaps a little less commonplace than mystery arising in relationship between two or more individuals (including animals) is the relationship like this, between individual and teacup. Individual and object. I will always remember when holding vigil at my father's deathbed, how strange the room looked to me as I grew increasingly attuned to any shift or change in his breath. Even the light switch was silently communicating its impermanence and fragility. It, like so many objects in my high school classrooms, seemed to pulse with atomic shimmer; only by invisible magic was the light switch holding together the dignity of its simple form. It broke my heart. The coils on the stovetop broke my heart. The pattern on the linoleum broke my heart. The stale fragrance of cigarette smoke from his last cigarettes broke my heart.

In *Transcendent: Art and Dharma in a Time of Collapse,* Curtis White writes of the Japanese term *mono no aware,* which refers to the gentle sadness or poignancy that arises with awareness of impermanence. He invokes the concept to contrast a more receptive way of being with the instrumental, efficiency-driven mentality dominating much of contemporary life. *Mono no aware* is not sentimental or dramatic but a kind of spacious pause from which we sense the passing nature of things and can provide a sense of the transcendent amid the everyday inventory of a modern life.

Here is Aimee Bender, on a flag:

I was very anxious; I was at the Faculty Club. I was not anxious due to being at the Faculty Club, but it didn't help. A big room, so many circular tables with cloth napkins, my own internal system flooded with static and panic as I'd set a deadline for myself to make a heavy decision about a relationship I was in. Why did I set such a hard deadline? In retrospect, I hadn't needed to, made it far worse for myself, but right then I was caught in the trap I'd made, vibrating with worry and indecision as the host led me to my table to meet with colleagues. Maybe it was a search committee lunch? I talked to others as if through a peephole while every thought forked into new anxious thoughts that jumbled and tumbled together as we ate our salads and drank our iced teas.

After the lunch, which I somehow managed to fake my way through, I sat outside on a small circular stone wall around a flagpole. It was a breezy spring day. I could go home, but I wasn't ready to, needed, in a way, to catch my breath. At the top of the pole was the bear on the California flag, fluttering. Out of a kind of desperation, I found myself focusing on that fluttering flag, watching its fabric bend and straighten with the wind. Bend and straighten, bend and straighten. Movement that was ongoing but also predictable to a degree. The waves and curves in the cloth responding to the breeze, contracting, expanding. Later, I would find out that this sort of attentiveness to a physical object is a classic grounding meditation exercise that's good for anxiety in particular, but I didn't know that then and was surprised to discover that as I sat there, wholly absorbed in the watching, I felt a little calmer. That my fractured scattered amped-up white noise of a self could pour out of me and into the flag. The wind moved around us both and shifted my hair and clothing.

—Aimee Bender, writer, Los Angeles, CA

THIS SOFTENING AND LOOSENING of self that Aimee writes of and that arises in relationship with the beauty of ordinary objects—it is not just a metaphysical idea, as Rabbi Rami Efal recently told me and a small group of students, but a lived invitation to let longing ripen without rushing it into action. When we hold that tension between ache and restraint, between immediacy and structure, being experience and [being] nothingness, everything we touch gains gravity. It is intimate, experiential, and relational. Then, too, here's Emerson again, with another consideration regarding the ordinary things, animals, trees, cities, war zones, landfills . . . populating the world around us: "We have learned that we do not see directly, but mediately, and that we have no means of correcting these colored and distorting lenses which we are, or of computing the amount of their errors. Perhaps these subject lenses have a creative power; perhaps there are no objects."[5]

–8–

Death and Dying

All goes onward and outward, nothing collapses,
And to die is different from what anyone supposed, and luckier.

—WALT WHITMAN, *Song of Myself*

I've had an unusual number of near-death experiences. In 1976, I was bitten by an alligator. In 2004, a nurse fed a bag of ciprofloxacin into my body. I was (and am) allergic to cipro. In 2017, I didn't understand that my appendix had burst, leaving me to scream through the night as the morphine did nothing until the surgeon and his team saved my life the next morning. In 2023, in an effort to see the whales beyond the Marietas Islands off Punta Mita in Mexico, the boat driver sped up before I was seated. My body flew, part of my skull cracking open when it hit the boat's console. I remembered nothing—of that moment, of hours before and hours since—until perhaps some eight to nine hours after the accident, my body in tremendous pain as my brother explained through my cell phone who I was, where I was, and what had happened.

But the experience of late summer 1994 was different. After almost four years of living and working in Miami Beach, I left that May for Munich. There I did summer-term coursework at Ludwig-Maximilians-Universität to strengthen my German language skills while visiting relatives. I returned to Miami Beach to pack, sell my car, and arrange to ship my belongings and myself to New York University and to the next chapter of my life.

On Saturday, August 13, two weeks before I'm to become a New Yorker, I attended a daytime wedding. It was a small, indoor affair in Hialeah, near the Miami Airport, the bride someone I had had a crush on years before. I attended by myself, having a sip of champagne when it was time to toast the couple and a glass of wine during the late lunch–early dinner. When I left, I immediately observed the morning clouds had given way to heavy, heavy rain, dulling what daylight shone through it.

I drove my Honda Civic SI along State Road 826, heading east as heavy rain fell on southern Florida. As I turned my steering wheel to connect to Interstate 95 at Miami's Golden Glades Interchange, my car didn't follow suit. Instead, I kept my former direction and drove off the curving on-ramp, some four-five-six stories above the ground. My fingernails dug into my steering wheel as my body locked. I saw only gray sky and elevated highways before me as my car and I left the ramp. When the car turned downward, I saw everyone I ever loved. My parents. My brother. My relatives, some passed but most still living. The first girl I ever loved. (My paternal grandfather had passed five years before; my maternal grandfather four years before. I hadn't seen that girl in over a year.) Almost thirty familiar, warm faces, panorama panning before me. They were all the color red, the gaps among them black. They all smiled back at me. I had no sense of time. I had no feelings of fear, none of worry.

My forehead almost hit the windshield. My seat belt held and worked. What I didn't see when I went over was the soil just below and beyond the ramp, also stories tall as it met the underside of the ramp. My car drove into it. Dampened by the day's rain, it swallowed the first yard or so of my car. My vision of loved ones vanished when the seat belt jerked my body back.

I sat in my car, shaken, frozen, feverish, grappling with what had happened and what could have happened. Without a sense of how much time had passed, I heard a tap on the window. A state trooper had slid down the soil. She asked if I was okay. A car had seen me go over and called. I didn't leave the car, not until the ramp was closed and a tow truck winched my car and me up and back onto the ramp.

With my other experiences, there was no flash of loving, in red or any color. Driving off that ramp—that was perhaps the one time I believed I was about to die. I can't account for what I saw in the midst of that belief. I was bruised but lucky not to have had any broken bones. A body shop repaired the damage to (mostly the underside of) my car and helped me find a buyer for it. I flew to La Guardia Airport and checked into New York University graduate student housing Sunday, August 28. And my life began anew.

—Beowulf Sheehan, artist and photographer, Kansas City, MO

DEATH, WHEN IT HAPPENS, is not an error or a failure; it is a rite of passage and a completion. There have been so many occasions when I have visited with a dying patient and/or their family to suggest these words, and the collective sigh, the relief they seem to feel at this shift in point of view, this little opening and loosening of their fear—it's palpable. These have often (though not always) been patients and families without active spiritual practices. "But," I've often heard in response, "we don't go to church." "Yeah," I would respond, "neither do I." Or, "But we don't believe in heaven." To which I'd say, "Nobody living knows what happens next—nobody."

In chapter 2, I mentioned that with Daishin, studying my life was studying my death. So it was and is. In Zen practice, the invitation is to stop running away from death and instead turn toward it. By the lights of our big, shared understanding, the dominant cosmovision, life is full of so-called problems to which some of us are constantly seeking solutions. Even mortality is seen by some as a problem to be solved, with cryogenics or by downloading the contents of our minds into alternative hardware as solutions rather than accepting mortality as a condition that bounds our aspirations and gives our lives meaning. Zhuangzi: "Why did you not simply lead him to see the unity of life and death, and that the admissible and inadmissible belong to one category, so freeing him from his fetters?"[1] Many Western philosophers feel likewise. Michel de Montaigne: "To philosophize is to learn how to die."[2] Tiokasin once told me that Westerners took everything from the Lakota except for one thing: "We still know how to die," he said.

It was unsurprisingly during this same Pacific season of lunches and dinners and student-teacher interviews with Daishin that I first underwent hospice training for volunteers. It was with Marsha Fox, the longest-serving president and CEO of VNAcare, a hospice organization in Southern California; she "worked" there for forty-seven years, and her training upended my life. I would not have eventually become a chaplain without meeting her, and someday I hope to lead a workshop that is half as graced as hers were. There are so many experiences from that weekend—a mere two days—that I could share. The most significant, I think, was swallowing a much larger dose of mortality salience than I'd experienced before. Mortality salience is that feeling you get when for a split second or two (maybe longer), you really get it—that you are mortal and you are going to die. That your minutes are limited; they are countable (though only by our survivors). Mortality salience punches you in the gut. Lights your hair on fire. You may briefly experience symptoms of physical shock. The blood may rush to your face. Your gaze may suddenly soften as you stare into the middle distance. It is utterly unlike accepting conceptually that one day you will die. There is talking about and describing and even smelling the tea, and there is briefly tasting the tea. Most of us, if my students over the years are any measure, have experienced mortality salience from time to time.

So if we are all indeed co-arising, and if co-arising involves awareness of a mutual calling to each other, then we must know that these calls will as often be calls of grief, suffering, and death as they will be calls of life, joy, and mutual celebration. And really, at this point in the twenty-first century, it can be hard to remember the life, joy, and celebration part of it all, especially if you still have a smartphone and a television. Almost certainly anyone with this book in hand and who has come as far as this page feels the injustices and shudders before even thirdhand reports of the horrors unfolding down the street, across the country and the pond. The world is filled with cruelty and sorrow that may have seemed unfathomable to many of us mere decades ago. If all of the experiences shared with me in making this book are mysterious, a number of them are decidedly dark, at least the following one is evil. The place from which truly evil human behavior springs has become so familiar, and the behavior so unfathomably abhorrent, my friend and colleague Ethan's experience may not register for you as unbelievable, even if clearly awful.

In 2022 I was living in Miami at a large apartment complex in a middle-class part of the city, with a tree-lined neighborhood next to our building, which was very concrete and not tree-lined. I would walk my dog, Libby (who has since passed away), back across the street into the neighborhood every day. In summer, we would usually not take too long, because it was hot and she was a big dog. But we would walk through lots of the tropical flora and fauna they have in Miami—lots of ferns and palms, plus tropical trees. Lizards were everywhere, especially in the summer, because they so thrive in that climate. One summer day, I took Libby back into the neighborhood, a little later in the morning than usual. There were lizards everywhere that would scatter from our feet. After we crossed the street, we passed a pretty grim-looking young guy. I think for some reason he gave me a little bit of a cold vibe, because I recall looking at him and he avoided eye contact. We continued on our walk on that side of the street for a few minutes, but I realized it was just too hot, so we turned back after maybe five or six minutes. Libby was very slow always, and we hadn't gone far, so we walked back along the same side of the street. I never saw or passed anyone else. As we got back to the place where we saw the guy, I noticed that right in the middle of the sidewalk there was a large, squashed lizard, probably about eight inches long, flat and with some blood showing. It had clearly been stomped on. I was really disgusted and upset by the sight—the lizards are totally harmless, and someone would really have to go out of their way to step that hard on a large lizard.

I thought about how many animals must have experienced this kind of horrible, malicious violence from humans, for no reason. I cried when I got back to the apartment, just thinking of the enormity of the problems that these creatures face, being so vulnerable to humans. The experience still haunts me, and I think it sort of hardened my resolve to try to help protect animals and resist these types of behaviors where possible. But it is hard to think about all those animals that have gone before and been lost in a moment of terror and pain like that. I don't know how they would feel in that circumstance, but I imagine they feel some kind of stress and fear at the very least—even lizards. So I grieve them. What else can we do?

—Ethan Prall, scholar and researcher, Houston, TX

DEEP GRIEF IS NOT EVIDENCE of pathology but of attachment, relation, and love. "When we love deeply," writes Dr. Joanne Cacciatore, "we mourn deeply; extraordinary grief is an expression of extraordinary love. Grief and love mirror each other; one is not possible without the other."[3] Ethan went home with Libby and wept. *What have I seen?* he wondered, crying. What *have I* seen? "Much of our disappointment about the way animals and nature are treated is centered on our fellow humans who act in ways that are sometimes scarcely believable," says environmental ethicist Dale Jamieson. And same for our disappointment about the way our fellow humans are treated.

I am a person who has caused all kinds of harm in my life so far, and I am troubled by my own unending greed and mean-heartedness—it's there every day, grinning at me. I try to acknowledge it without enacting it, though I'm not always successful; I have a full spectrum of human potential in me and have learned that as soon as I think I'm above behaving a certain way, I am most vulnerable to it. And still, we continue to witness in this world human action that it is essentially impossible for me to imagine performing. It can really impress upon me the same wonder and feeling of being dumbstruck as I am by a sunset or a moonrise. Most of us—the vast majority of people I know—I think do not speak or act from this place.

Ethan—Dr. Prall—has gone on to dedicate his life to the protection of animals. That is one kind of a choice a person can make when blown away by evil. *Easy for him*, you might say. But "love and compassion are necessities, not luxuries," the Dalai Lama writes in *The Art of Happiness*. "Without them, humanity cannot survive."[4]

To bear witness, especially to human behavior, and to sense and feel deeply the life around us is to see and experience suffering, cruelty, and incomprehensible destruction. Life is a miracle and an atrocity. Once, as a new hospital chaplain, I was working on a Friday night and received a page to visit a patient in the Trauma Burn Unit. As I would learn, the individual, who had experienced a lifetime of injustices, cruelty, and ill treatment within the institutions presumably designed to help them, had at last doused themselves with gasoline and lit themselves on fire. Because it was a Friday, the Spiritual Care office was empty and dark. There was one other staff chaplain there, thank goodness—a long-timer whose experience and warmth I trusted. Before going down to see the patient, I asked her, somewhat facetiously and nervously, "Ever had a patient who lit themselves on fire but did not die?" Calmly, making complete and direct eye contact, she answered, "Yes." Many times, her response and expression told me—even in our midsize and relatively affluent city. I asked her if she had any advice. Her response was something like, "Go there and meet them there," or "Go there and be there."

I know what it feels like to be pilloried, with my head and hands restrained, in a public space, as punishment. In shame. I remembered the experience, once. It came out of nowhere and overcame me and then was gone. In it, I was female, and my mouth was bound. It was a Total. Horror. I only remembered this a single time but it haunts me. I am terrified of the feeling of it and hope I never feel it again. At the same time, I will never totally forget it.

—Anonymous, Los Angeles, CA

A MIRACLE AND AN ATROCITY. If you close the window to one, you're closing the window to both. "To love," writes psychotherapist Francis Weller, "is to accept the rites of grief."[5] Eventually every one of us will lose everything. My maternal grandmother led a beautiful life and died peacefully at ninety-three. By then, except for her children and grandchildren, she had lost practically everything she'd ever owned, except what fit in her small assisted-living apartment, and everyone she'd ever known and loved: her grandparents, parents, aunts and uncles, cousins, every one of her twelve siblings (including in-laws), all of her friends (her social network was a women's club of much younger women), her husband of fifty-nine years—everyone. And experiencing loss is not the kind of thing we grow increasingly casual about the more we experience it; rather, pain intensifies with each new loss—especially, I would venture, if we are living fully. Loss has a way of sharpening, not dulling, our focus and awareness. Though I never asked her about it specifically, I could see, and I remember, that every new loss for my grandmother was poignant and painful, even as she knew that life and the world would continue, mercilessly, no matter her losses. And hers was what we consider a blessed, very lucky situation because she'd lived long enough to lose that much. There is mystery here.

In the aforementioned college course on death and dying I once cotaught, we held a fairly well-known guided meditation about death. Each student begins with twenty small slips of paper separated into four piles, putting five slips in each category: possessions or material objects of importance; things of value in nature or the world; important activities; and beloved people or animals. The facilitator—in the classroom, me or my coteacher—then begins talking the class through a terminal diagnosis and subsequent steps of pain, fatigue, isolation, ultimate withdrawal from the world, and death. Along the way, at certain points, students have to consider, weigh, and toss one or two slips of paper into the middle of the room, giving each of them up, forever; at one point, one of us would take a piece of paper right out of their pile, without their opportunity to choose. It's a very powerful exercise, and I'll never forget the look on one student's face as she slowly lifted her head, which was piled in her arms on her desk, and pointed her tearful eyes at us: "I thought at the end there would be something left!"

While we're alive, the more we're aware to how many relationships comprise us—extending further than our imaginations can reach and including trillions of beneficial bacteria, fungi, and viruses in our own guts—the more we realize our contingency and the impossibility of fundamental independence and, perhaps, the more we begin to feel pain "out there" within our own being. It is curious to me that awakening to emptiness—this lack of any fixed or permanent self or essence to anything or anyone—should somehow almost automatically entail *more* tenderness and sensitivity, but it absolutely does. If you just think about this contingency and emptiness, you may feel nihilistic. But when you experience it, the only possible response is kindness. Says George Saunders, "Kindness is the only non-delusional response to the human condition."[6] Awakening aside, it only takes badly hurting or mistreating someone once to know how true it is that hurting another is hurting yourself. I once knew a man who had a long history of deliberately exploiting and abusing people—it was serious, and in at least one case that I know of, it was criminal. I think somehow he couldn't stop himself. He had a system and it worked. But occasionally, unpredictably, he would be hit with what he called "the horrors" about his life and behavior. He would lock himself in his room and cry, and loathe upon himself, and stop eating, and punish himself for days until the horrors subsided. If you're looking for good reasons to stick with the dominant cosmovision, the illusion of self-protection is probably pretty enticing.

Because, in fact, a more relational worldview in which one is inseparable from the rest of the world and its happenings may sound in some respects like a fairy tale, but it may also feel like a horror story, depending on what it is you're witnessing and what is co-arising. Who wants to experience themselves as inseparable from a starving child? Or an assassin? Or an unhoused addict dying on the sidewalk? As an autocrat bombing innocent people? Or indeed, as those very innocent people? Sounds like a good way to get oneself hurt or very, very depressed. Indeed, it may even seem from the vantage point of the twenty-first century that survival requires we freeze out totally experiences more aligned with a relational way of being. That we understand each of us is separate, isolated, perhaps well-resourced, and safe from the effects of the conditions of climate change, for example. This might mean certain things about your portfolio, if you have one. It might mean—not to mention billionaire bunkers too much—that you're a person who wants to install a sniper tower on your Greenwich, Connecticut, mansion in preparation for end-times, or that you are among a group of super-wealthy considering putting "disciplinary collars" on your hired help so that they don't mutiny during apocalypse.[7]

But I would imagine that if you feel empathy at all—if you register and feel any kind of pain when another is suffering—this bunker/sniper-tower stance wouldn't go smoothly for you. You'd have to dispense with empathy altogether if you could, as engaging it is a surefire way to feeling yourself toward a more relational cosmovision, which you'd want to avoid at all costs (and sounds like you can spend a lot) if your personal survival were the foremost and perhaps single guiding feature of your life. In any case, though, sorry not sorry; you are doomed, just like the rest of us. As the French philosopher Edgar Morin explains in *Homeland Earth*:

> The awesome cosmos is itself doomed. Having been born, it is mortal. It expands at a maddening speed, as stars collide, explode, and implode. Our Sun, the successor to two or three other defunct suns, will itself burn out. All living beings are thrown into life without being asked and are destined for death without having wished it. They live between nothingness and nothingness, the one behind us, the other ahead, all the while surrounded by nothingness. It is not only individuals who are doomed, but, sooner or later, humankind, then the last traces of life, and finally the Earth. The cosmos itself is running to its death, whether

> through scattering itself in all directions or through returning implosively to its origin. From this dead cosmos perhaps another will rise, but our cosmos will then be irredeemably dead.[8]

We must somehow take a wider view, look at the whole landscape, really see it, and describe what's going on here. Then we can at least wail the right question into the swaddling band of darkness, or, if it comes to that, choir the proper praise.[9] With most things under investigation in the Western world, we like to "start with what we know." Why shouldn't it also be so in our investigations into the nature of being? I find that Perdita Finn and Edgar Morin's insights regarding pretty much all we know for sure about existence (and so which might guide us in understanding our purpose or at least the best use of our time) pair together beautifully. Here is a refrigerator list for you:

1. "Darkness and mystery surround us on all sides."[10]
2. "We are apparently lost in the cosmos. No one knows how we got here—earth, life, humanity, and consciousness appear to be the temporary outcome of a literally unfathomable series of events."[11]
3. "We are wandering. We do not tread a well-marked path. We can no longer use the law of progress as radar."[12]
4. "Humanity is part of a community of life."[13]
5. "Humanity's destiny cannot be separated from the destiny of the Earth itself."[14]
6. "Everybody will die without exception. This is not a failure, and it's not a mistake."[15]
7. "The Earth and the Sun themselves will die, dragging life along with them. But to these already envisioned deaths must be added new, more intimate ones, new global deaths, a looming, enveloping . . . series of deaths weighing on the planet as a whole."[16]

–9–

Grief

At one time I thought it was strange and miraculous to have meaningful communication with a nonhuman animal, interaction where we recognized each other's personhood. In recent decades, it seems normal. Of course animals are people, and if I can sit quietly enough to let them know I see them—that is, that I see their personhood—it makes sense that some of them might sit quietly enough to let me know they see me, too.

More recently, the past five years or so, the surprise has been that trees are people. I've come to understand this gradually, but with increasing urgency. At first I was seeing them as individuals and that was interesting and comforting, but then I read more about them and I began to understand a forest as a collective or community or a many-souled organism, trees interconnected through the air and underground, trees raising young ones around them, protecting them but also forcing them to fight through the canopy for sunlight, thereby making them strong. I began thinking about American forests, which used to grow shore to shore, and how we massacred whole civilizations of them, nearly all of them.

My husband and I had a giant post oak outside our house. It toppled over in the night, to our grief. In its place we planted four new trees. For a while I was so pleased, seeing them out there. I followed the watering instructions, rooted for them, but then one day I was standing outside taking pictures of them, and I suddenly understood them as freakishly alone and suffering. It was as though they said it. Not a sentence but as if they were emitting a sensation or a sound, as if I heard their cry of confusion and disorientation and alienation. A sort of buzzing, a cacophony that swept through, and I saw: They were born in a nursery and stuck in the ground, not knowing what their job was, no community, no connection, so contrary to their kingdom's evolution. They just hang there, with no language, the language of their ancestors destroyed. They are refugees, ornaments, zoo creatures. They will always be lost and weak, never learn their tribe's vanished traditions and wisdom. To see them any other way is a lie that we tell ourselves in order to live with our choices. I think we all know it, deep down, that the story runs deep, does not stop at chickens in cages and pigs in pens.

—Deb Olin Unferth, novelist, Chicago, IL

"PROGRESS LOOKS LIKE BOWING TO LIFE'S SORROWS AND BETRAYALS," Father Gregory Boyle teaches in *Tattoos on the Heart.*[1] And indeed, sometimes it seems someone or something bigger than us would have us acknowledge and absorb that the "point" of being here—whatever we are, wherever we are—is to be as grief-stricken and heartbroken as possible. What other, better measure that we loved hard and well? Is it or will it be painful if, as other myths of progress collapse, we find ourselves resonating with or finding meaning in seeing the world as deeply and fundamentally relational? No doubt. Exquisitely painful and exquisitely sad. It may also be that being a fully mature human in this and any age involves allowing oneself to grieve and mourn without "getting better" or "getting over it." Rather, as Ethan Prall shared with us, when the appropriate response is to grieve, just grieve. So much easier said than done in our culture.

This was a few years ago. I was in the forested hills of the Driftless region in southwest Wisconsin, in *sesshin* (silent retreat) at Great Plains Zen Center in late summer, staying in an orange tent near the northern red oak (colloquially called the Minnesota red oak) that was planted when I was *shuso* (or "head trainee," a yearlong post). Everything was yellow. Goldenrod, daisies, black-eyed Susans, tall prairie grasses that were beginning to soften from the brilliant greens of midsummer to the color of oats. It was almost the end of the week—a Thursday night—when I woke up just before midnight and did something I've never done in all my years as a student: I snuck into the kitchen to get some food. Specifically, I made myself a bowl of cereal. I brought it out to my tent and ate it cross-legged in the dark, thinking, *This is something Chrissie would do.* My little sister, Chrissie. She was always walking on tiptoe into the kitchen for another bowl of cereal. I never ate cereal.

In the morning, my mom called and told me my little sister had unfathomably, unexpectedly, and suddenly died the night before. She had undiagnosed, untreated fibroids, and during a heavy menstrual cycle, she bled to death in her living room in her sleep (though we would not know this until the autopsy was completed, several months later). The last thing she did on this planet before falling asleep was braid her daughter's hair. There was an unfinished cup of tea and a notebook on the table beside the couch where my brother-in-law found her, half toppled onto the floor. We all wondered if she'd known she was in trouble and was trying to get up, for help.

And we were all shattered. She was forty-two, mother of a soon-to-be-sixteen-year-old daughter who had recently received an organ donation. Chrissie was a loving wife, a pediatric patient advocate, and a jazz singer. She was one hundred days newly sober. In the days and weeks that followed her death, I would go home to Ohio, stand next to my mom for six hours at Chrissie's wake—my older sister, Carrie, was too devastated to stand there with us or indeed to ever look at her body—while over five hundred people lined up to pay their last respects. Neighbors, old friends, cousins, aunts, uncles, and so many beloved strangers. Over five hundred people is a *lot* of people. The entire time, my body was in a biochemical state of fight or flight: shaking legs, loose knees, heat racing up and down my front, then back, in a horrible sequence I saw in my mind making a dark, red ellipse. Then I stood with my mom and big sister during the funeral service, holding my mother's hand, stroking Carrie's hair. Then I was doubled over at the end of the service as the bagpipes played "Amazing Grace." Then I was in my mom's backyard, full of relatives, full of cake, full of cards and so many fucking flowers. Then I was looking out over the fence, into the dense trees behind the property, thinking of all the late summers I had known, this was the latest summer.

In two days I would return home to Minnesota and sixty hours a week of work, preparation for Zen priesthood ordination, six-year-old twin boys, and a coping routine I'd learn from grief counseling called a short-term energy-relieving behavior, or STERB:[2] I ran seven to ten miles each afternoon; I ate a lot of noodles (about a pound of them daily—spaghetti, sweet potato noodles, buckwheat noodles, rice noodles, bean noodles . . .); I drank red wine (a couple glasses with dinner); and I slept ten to twelve hours a night, more if I could get away with it. Every waking hour was in a world I did not recognize; I had made all of my commitments and vows and knew everything and everyone in a world that Chrissie lived in. It was not as if, but was actually the case that the entire net of relations in this fabric that comprises all of us . . . it changed fundamentally. It was January before the STERB strategy broke down and grief really took me by the throat.

What I didn't know about grief, though I'd experienced many losses of all kinds—a divorce, multiple pregnancy losses, death of my father and many family members and friends—was fundamental and familiar to anyone, I would guess, who really explores their relationship to loss. I did not know until this string of January nights how all of my accumulated grief and innumerable and erstwhile unnamed losses were situated along the same nerve—an actual physical nerve that ran straight through the center of my body with a racing heat that felt like fire. And that when a sudden traumatic loss—Chrissie's death—touched that nerve, everything stored along it, unacknowledged and unmourned for years, began to wail and sing.

The accumulated losses howled in me in the middle of the night, during the darkest, coldest days of the year in Minnesota, disrupting the hours and hours of slumber I'd initially been banking up every night since Chrissie died, robbing me. *Bereaved*: The word comes to us from the Old English word *berēafian*, which means "to deprive of" and is related to *reave*, or "to rob."

Nothing would quiet the howls, for nothing could restore what had been stolen from us, and suddenly I could not sleep. My new task, it seemed, was not to carry on as though everything would be or already was okay; it was to hold vigil every night, night after night, calling up, reviewing, and reliving every imaginable loss I'd ever experienced—loss of youth, of innocence, of hope, of security. Of my childhood home, my first school, my best friend in kindergarten who moved away to Texas, to my first lover, after college, who I finally realized had never loved me. The losses were biological, emotional, psychological, financial, real, imagined . . . I was wide awake, and I could see and feel, it seemed, each and every one, as if finally making up for the days, weeks, months, and years I had spent turning away from or not even noticing them.

Nothing helped. Not running more by day, with YakTrax strapped to the bottoms of my tennis shoes for running over ice. Not a glass of wine more, or none at all. Not anxiety medication or antidepressants or sleeping aids. Not more zazen. Not a Tangaryo (all-day silent meditation). Not koan study and *definitely* not my Zen teacher telling me the story of Kisa Gautami, the bereaved mother who carried her dead child from house to house begging for someone to please bring the child back to life, whom the Buddha tasked with finding one house in the countryside that had not experienced such loss—a process of reflecting on suffering and impermanence that with the swift magic of sudden awakening, somehow jolted her awake. Her awakening I believe, but I doubted then, when told to consider her story, and still doubt today that Kisa Gautami's grief disappeared. Grief is not like that, and anyway, many thoughts, emotions, and human desires persist amid a lifetime of awakening. We are human, after all.

Music did not help; indeed, it was unbearable. Nor did audiobooks. Nor white noise. And it wasn't just grief—it wasn't just sadness. It was panic; it was shame; it was every negative feeling nudged awake by sharp awareness of the passage of time and my own vulnerability and nature, as a human, to be wrong, to make mistakes, to seriously mess up. Every perceived shortcoming or moral failure I'd ever experienced danced across the screen of my mind in vivid detail. Over and over and over. It was a nightmare.

My day "job" during this season was threefold. First, as a research fellow for the Harvard Animal Law and Policy Program, I was helping research and write a massive, fifteen-country study of animal markets and zoonotic disease. Pandemic—a feature of the Anthropocene we are only beginning to reckon with—had brought with it racism and finger-pointing that we hoped our study would dispel; every country in the world, and none more so than the United States, uses and consumes animals in vast network of animal markets.[3]

The work brought me to some very dark places: inside slaughterhouses where annually 330,000 pigs arrive already dead and 800 million pigs arrive unable to walk due to a lifetime of torture and fatal transportation via trucks on interstates;[4] into small ships sailed close to the shore up around the Horn of Africa, in which kidnapped infant wildlife, women, and children, alongside weapons, are trafficked north.[5]

I hadn't known until I was immersed in this research that in a single year, the United States legally imports more than 224 million live wild animals and 883 million wildlife products worth over $4.3 billion. That in addition, over 22 million living livestock animals are imported into the United States for consumption, alongside the 10 billion livestock and poultry animals already raised in-country, in factories. (If we round down to 10 billion animals slaughtered annually in the United States for food, that's 317 animals per second.) I did not know that parrots are stuffed into socks and ziplock bags and primates and big cats are drugged then stored in trunks of cars or in boxes labeled "washing machine." That in some cases, animals are transported and sold alive to restaurants where they are kept living in cages in hidden rooms so that customers can select and kill, fresh, the animal they want to consume for dinner. That in order to catch wild birds, trappers and poachers will superglue a live captive bird to a tree, enticing highly socialized birds to come and visit, whereupon the visiting birds are captured, too. That live animals sold through vendors at animal markets are shipped on motorbikes, on cargo boats, or through the US mail. That supply-and-demand dynamics move animals of hundreds of species—many of them young, stolen from nests and dens—across states, nations, and continents, transported in backpacks, piled in boxes, on barges, and hitched onto the side of motorbikes. I did not know that during the day, while I was making lunches, logging into work, washing dishes, or scrolling on my phone . . . that impoverished and starving hunters and poachers desperate to support their families were capturing then selling billions of individual animals, who were transported and laundered along a value chain that ended more frequently in the United States than in any other country, where humans would consume these billions of individual animals both living and dead, including their body tissues and parts such as skin, bones, organs, and blood; for game or bushmeat; as trophies; as live exotic pets; as commercial products such as toys and household decorations, and employing body parts otherwise consumed as food or used for ritual, religious, and/or medicinal use. I did not know that at every hour of every day, the legal and illegal wildlife trades extend across local, national, and international regions and markets, transporting animals by hand in nets and bags, on bicycles, motorcycles, via truck, taxis and buses, hidden in boxes and containers in vehicle trunks and on cargo planes, in small boats and on freighters.[6] Now I do know, and so do you. Please try not to put those rocks back in place as they sat before the beginning of this paragraph.

Another part-time job was coteaching that class on death and dying at Carleton College, which was down the street from me at the time, and where I was visiting professor of ethical inquiry. My coteacher and I were trying to make discussion about old age, sickness, and death less taboo. We talked about DNRs, advanced directives, living wills. We talked about the meaning of life, about telic and atelic values, and we read Atul Gawande and the Stoics and Borges and Emily Dickinson. We tried gently every week to coax alive a little fragile mortality salience among ourselves in hopes that awareness of death might somehow improve the relationship our students (and we) had to an ever-diminishing number of days alive on an Earth experiencing mass extinction and life-extinguishing effects of climate change. Though on the whole these classes were wonderful, it could of course sometimes get a little grim and intense. Moreso than we'd expected, my colleague and I had to address features of the Anthropocene, such as climate change, because they were on students' minds. We could not, with their generation, discuss death, dying, and loss without addressing what it meant to be navigating an age characterized by such pervasive and complete human dominance over the planet. Nor, at this point, can anyone.

Once, amid a rigorous class discussion about end-of-life decisions and care and their intersection with ecological grief, a student raised his hand and asked, "If everything we hear is happening to the planet is really happening, shouldn't addressing it urgently be all that we're doing? Like, we shouldn't be doing anything else? Not even this? Is this as catastrophic an emergency as it seems?"

Each of those students, and each of us, faces these questions, and not just once but many times we must make a decision about how to live in response to them. There is much opportunity for curious people in such questions—there especially was in a class in which we were encouraging each other to explore and talk about what it means to be mortal. There may be, we told our students, no more poignant era than this one in which to confront our thoughts and feelings about loss. According to Dale Jamieson,

> The Anthropocene . . . threatens virtually everything we care about. The Anthropocene will mean unnecessary suffering, early death, and extinction for many people and animals. It will threaten the persistence of values, cultures, and ways of life that constitute the foundations of a meaningful life. Climate change (and other expressions of the Anthropocene) will remake the world, rupture our time horizons, erode our commitments to long-term projects, and damage our hopes for our children and their futures. The existential risk of climate change engages one of the most primeval fears of humanity: the fear of chaos and disorder. In threatening cultural death, it confronts us with the terrifying fact of our own inevitable demise.[7]

Ironically, the last regular job I was holding down that season was freelance editing and proofreading for a fixed income management company, which I was on the clock for several hours a week. I loved my coworkers there, and they remain dear to me. They were warm, had integrity, and my longtime manager Caroline Catalan in particular demonstrated exquisite leadership and always put our families and nonwork lives first. I can only imagine how difficult that was to manage. I consider her today a dear friend whose flexibility allowed me to be, pre-COVID, the only work-from-home employee in a firm operating across five continents. Hats off to all such decent human beings in managerial positions at such enormous corporate firms.

But. The language and context of this job were more fictional, more make-believe, more fantastical than even the novel I was working on in stolen minutes each day. Everything about the language for and the financial markets themselves seemed to me built of and upon elaborate fictional beliefs, fictional projections, simulations, abstract symbols detached from the material world, and self-referential loops of densely coded communication for an elite club. Don't get me wrong—despite the abstract and speculative nature of this world (not incidentally one of the three pillars of a one-world world), its *effects* are visible, measurable, and profound; and I experience daily my lack of reverence for all that. By the hour, though, I edited sentences about the consumer sentiment index, GDP, federal interest rates, agency-backed mortgages. And it was a system that was sickeningly, undeniably dependent upon its baked-in incentives for environmental destruction. I drafted and edited sentences with no actual referents in the world except the extent to which they manifest as obscene wealth for a very few, and all the impacts of *that*, which we could do worse than define with Jamieson's observations about the Anthropocene. This position provided practically all of my income for more than a decade after completing a postdoc in English. It was an untaxed, no-benefits, hourly-wage job in which I felt, somehow, safer and freer than I would have in an English department. Which is not to say I fully embrace my younger self and all her decisions.

There are many ways I am a servant of a culture I despise, as the philosopher Jack Turner's brilliant *The Abstract Wild* puts it, but perhaps never so much as in the days when I could read and read and read and read, and continue writing and publishing fiction, and start a family, by hiding out at home as a financial proofreader. It also enabled me to travel to and from my Zen teachers, and to pause in silent retreat schedules when I needed to work, because even though these were the only vacations I took for many, many years, I was, again, a contract worker without benefits and took breaks and days off to my own detriment. It was a decade-plus that was nothing if not totally irresponsible by most measures of modern life. There's no external validator of a life. None, for anyone. Not making money, I can't even pretend to have one.

I did not write anything, however, during this winter of three jobs and amid grieving my sister. I did not read "for fun," I did not watch TV, I did not hang out with friends. I did not consume sugar. I did not drink wine or eat noodles. I did not run outside. And I did not sleep.

I discovered the right medicine by accident. Downstairs, next to a tall window, we had a giant beanbag—big enough for three or four adults to sit on simultaneously. And every night, curled up in the middle of it because his legs were too weak to get him up and down the stairs reliably, was Snoop.

Snoop was a dog we had not been looking for but who found us in a park one day. The local Prairie's Edge Humane Society was there with all their adoptable dogs, and my husband and I were there with our boys. We stopped to greet the animals—of course we did!—and by that point in the afternoon, there was only one animal unclaimed. It was Snoop. He was twelve or thirteen. Old. He'd been a stray in southern Minnesota, and while it should have been easy for his family to claim him, such as the circumstances were, no one claimed him. And for months, no one adopted him, either. So, he was moved up to Rice County where we were living to try a different group of humans. Half his teeth were rotted, and his breath was awful, though he'd had extensive dental care with the Humane Society. His eyes were bleary, his muzzle was gray, he waddle-limped instead of running or walking, and he was the sweetest, gentlest dog. We spent a little time with him, thanked the folks who had him but let them know we weren't looking for a dog, and we went home. Later that night, my husband and I looked at each other: We didn't know why, but we needed that dog. So, in two days, I brought him home.

At the time of writing, it's been about two years since having ushered Snoop out of this world with my children and a traveling vet, two years after having buried his remains and planted flowers and incense over them. Snoop came to us as beat up, lonely, and broken as an old dog can be—and that's how I found him on the beanbag one night that January, snoring away with his stinky breath. I curled up next to him. And every subsequent night for months, that was where I slept through the night. I had to have at least one hand touching Snoop at all times, and somehow, not despite all the grief and regret singing in me but amid it, I could rest.

Though I still can't say precisely what was happening between me and Snoop on that old beanbag island (truly like a giant zafu), beat-up but comfortable, resting together, I know that we were moral and spiritual equals, and that on that beanbag, Snoop and I were in the kind of relationship where he did not expect me to be cheerful, productive, a good sleeper, or asleep at all. He did not want treats or food or a walk. I did not expect his breath to stop stinking or for him to stop snoring or farting. There was nothing to say and nothing to understand. There was nowhere to walk, nothing to dig, nothing to fetch, no squirrels to stalk; no work for me to do, dishes to wash, children to tend, research to undertake. I maybe hummed a little to him or scratched his ears or patted his enormous old belly, but we did not talk about our sorrows. We did not talk at all. We slept. Night after night like that. In dreams that season, I searched for all my dogs, loved and lost over the years: Abbey, Clyde, Monster, Truck. I found them all—in forests, at rest stops, underfoot, out back. When I found them in dreams, not memories of them but them actually, I would reach out and touch them, reassured. And I slept and slept.

Again, Joanne Cacciatore, or Dr. Jo as she is called: "To fully inhabit grief is to hold the contradictions of the great mystery that loss shatters us and we become whole. Grief empties us and we are filled with emotion. Fear paralyzes us and we lend courage to another. We mourn our beloveds' absence and we invoke their presence. We cease to exist as we once were and we become more fully human."[8]

Eventually, I found my way to Dr. Jo's place, Selah Carefarm, in northern Arizona—a sanctuary for abused, tortured, and neglected animals as well as for humans suffering as the result of traumatic loss. In this space I discovered that my experience with Snoop was one instance of a clinically profound practice occurring there regularly and by design. At Selah Carefarm, human and nonhuman animals are not only considered morally equal but spiritually equal as well. If you think this is a crazy idea, let me tell you: It is not an idea. When you are in such an intentional place, where healing is a natural outcome of simply existing together with many grief-stricken creatures, it is easily realizable. In this space, in which our relational interdependence is as raw and undeniable as our losses, it is the animals who are the chaplains. I say this not casually or cavalierly but with the utmost sincerity and seriousness. Dr. Jo, who knows of what she speaks, told me: "Animals are healers. They don't ask us to explain our pain. They sit with us in silence, offering presence, which is often the most powerful medicine."

At that artists' gathering in Plum Village I mentioned on page 6, every day we took long, silent walks in meditation over the beautiful, forested grounds, and it was so rainy and fecund and fragrant. Loss, like love, can never be understood—only experienced. And on one of these days, I experienced again, as if it were the same initial fresh shock, the death of my little sister. It is hard to type those words. There is an invisible pause in this paragraph between the last sentence and this one that took several minutes. There, at Plum Village, barefoot among the trees, I was desperate—just desperate—to take her hand one more time, to hear her actual voice—just once more—tears streaming as I walked. And I knew, thank God for my many teachers, I knew, that the closest I would ever get to her was to feel totally—*totally*—my bare feet on the earth.

She'd texted me a joke about chickens in the wilderness on a trail she was hiking on. The next day, she'd accidentally dialed me and I could hear, faintly, a conversation she was having. A text later that evening was "Sorry, butt-dial." A day later, her husband contacted me saying that I should call him because she was having trouble putting together words. Followed by the dire diagnosis, and not even a week later, a brain hemorrhage, and then a weird limbo between when her advanced directive kicked in and the message that she was gone. Couldn't have been a week and a half between chicken jokes and that horrible message.

It was October 2020, so funerals were out of the question. I wandered the rocky Alaska beach that I still traverse just about every week. I walked and if there were tears, I didn't feel them in the cold wind coming off the glaciers and snow-laden mountains. There's a large flat rock, about a mile down the beach, maybe a little more, and I sat on it that day to listen to the waves turning over the graywacke cobbles and to talk with her, the friend who I would never text with about chickens again.

The sounds of the stones and the waves, the sharp smell of the salt water and the wrack line, and the capacity of the ocean to hold it all let me breathe deeply and give a little of my confusion and anger and deep wrenching sorrow to the wind. For the first time since her death, I felt held, solid, like a great hand was holding me in place so that I could let myself say goodbye. And just as the words left my lips, an amazing thing happened: A harbor seal lifted her head from the water about fifteen feet away from me.

She just bobbed there. Or he. Who knows? But her large liquid eyes held my gaze for the longest time. I felt seen—not by my missing friend but by another creature who could meet my sorrow without flinching. As if the world knew that I needed someone to see me as my friend had seen me. After about ten incredible minutes, the seal slipped under, and I put my hands in my pockets and headed back toward the parking area. Then a man walking toward me on the beach started shouting and pointing at the water, and sure enough the seal was following me. Inordinately close to the shore, very unlike seals in this part of Alaska. She followed me all the way to where

I would peel off and head inland. Then she slipped back into the gray waves and I've never seen a seal on that part of the bay again.

—Erin Coughlin Hollowell, poet, executive director of Storyknife Writers Retreat, Syracuse, NY

My grandfather spoke different languages even in English. He was well traveled like his sons. All saw war and came back as they were. This was their path, their journey, for our generations. I went into several battles of my own, unaware and unsure of how I would get through the journey. It involved becoming too close with death. Navajo tradition tells us not to become too close to death as it would render one vulnerable, almost susceptible to all that is negative and dark in this world. It would create a need to restore Hózhó (balance), which is why when warriors return home we perform Diné Hózhóójí, or the Navajo Blessing Way Ceremony—which is spiritually bound to Navajo creation stories told since the beginning of time and specifically rooted to Changing Woman and her twin warrior sons. Should one not go through the Blessing Way Ceremony after war, they would continue their lives in darkness and chaos that renders them susceptible to evil.

I've never shared this story before mainly because Navajo people in general are quiet about their spirituality. When my grandfather passed away, my uncle, James Jr., told me to stay up all night and he would pick me up in the morning before dawn. When the stars were still in the sky he took me to a baseball field and had a coffee can of ashes from the fireplace in his hand. We faced east and began to pray in English and Navajo, and we poured rows of ashes on the cold ground. A medicine man instructed him to do this with me because he was the eldest and I was the youngest in the whole family. He told him to do this so my grandfather will remain in the afterlife. My grandfather fought in the Korean War, and his two sons served in Vietnam. I remember one Christmas after returning home from college, my uncle Jason told me to come over, and we sat down on the living room floor in front of the fireplace. He asked me if everything was okay because something seemed off about me. This was when I was eighteen years old, so I had just graduated high school, and during the last year of high school I lost friends and cousins to murders, suicides, and overdoses. Let's just say I buried a lot of close ones that year, a year that is meant for celebration and transition. I just wanted to get out alive.

The fireplace crackled with lively fireflies of sparks seeming to fissure into opposite ways as they ascended. We sat there on the floor with his wife, waves of orange hues flickering on each others' faces. Jason turned down the pro-wrestling commentating on the TV to a whisper and lit cedar and juniper in an abalone shell, and together we prayed. His hands, rough, jagged, weathered, and worn, cradled mine. He began to pray in Navajo and in English while waving the smoke from head to toe. His wife lit some mountain tobacco wrapped in a corn husk, and together we prayed. He then took out a small leather pouch from his pocket. Inside was corn pollen. He took a pinch of it, placed some on top of my head, and made a cross on my forehead with the rest of it. I then took a pinch and placed it on my tongue and prayed for my safety away from home. He then tied the small pouch and gave it to me and told me anytime I feel scared or need safety to say these prayers in this way. These are stories of our generations, from beginning to end.

Anatomy of the Southwest

Blood of Ye'iitsoh, Grants, NM

Two brothers, lightning in one hand,
Arrows in the other.
Nothing biblical in the creation of this story.
A giant, a monster spreading famine
Like manna in the desert—
Like sons searching for fathers.

That monster, an ardent comet,
A feverish fountain—spewing
Angry flashes of blood.
The twin warriors storm the mountain
Harnessed with lightning for weapons.
Defeated, the monster sleeps, casted in a blackened crust.

Contact, Winslow, AZ

Striping the auburned sky with a razor's edge tailing for a millennium,
The comet impacts crusted Indigenous floors
Ripping layers of sediment—
Delicate grains uprooted in splashes.
Mantled armored plates shiv like a hand through your chest,
A hand canoed through hearts.

As Cedar Embers in Abalone Shell, Gobernador Knob, NM

Through four worlds
Endless turquoise stones emerge
Through folds of claret soil
Creating Seasonal Woman—
A birth, a breath.
Life, endless.

Woman of early light,
Footsteps sealed in clay,
Children follow her way,
The circle budding from earth;
The sun blooms in stillness
Corn pollen kisses one child to the next.

Seasonal Woman, The State of Hózhó, Dinétah
Woman of four seasons:
Her presence fires leaves;
Her presence fastens currents;
Her presence seeps breath from root to limb—
Her presence fills the lungs of our days.
Her presents—the foliage of the sacred circle.

Woman of endless life born, and reborn.
Cyclical patterns, webbed etchings—
The palm of a hand, the footprint and face of our daughters
Raised to be mothers. giving breath to children of the earth—
Inhaled and exhaled, life within us
Compresses; it expands.
It compresses and it expands.

—Kyle Wilson, poet, Fort Defiance, AZ

-10-
Responsibility

Complete, mature human beings are devoted to making a difference for others.

—WENDY EGYOKU NAKAO, personal interview

Loving human beings build loving societies resting on the web of mutuality. A world where every world fits, the Zapatistas say. The diversity of our tribes is our superpower.

—FATHER GREGORY, *The Whole Language*

The purpose of every life is to grow in wisdom and learn to love better.

—FRANK, *The Five Invitations*

In 2021 I was doing a five-day, virtual meditation retreat led by Kittisaro and Thanissara of Sacred Mountain Sangha. Something that I've noticed about long periods of meditation is that over the course of a few days, the "monkey mind" that wants to dodge and dart on anything other than the meditative task at hand . . . gives up. The monkeys come down from the trees where they'd been jabbering and sit on the ground exhausted. Toward the end of the retreat, I was sitting with a cup of tea during a break and I looked at the cup and it seemed to pulse. I groaned, thinking, *Oh man, now what?*

The focus of the retreat was the Buddhist figure Kuan Yin (or Avalokiteshvara), the bodhisattva of compassion. I was not yet comfortable with thinking of these figures in the Mahayana pantheon as in any sense real, and I kept asking and wondering, "Kittisaro, what do you mean by Kuan Yin? Are you saying that she is a real being? A personification of something? A metaphor? What?" My rational mind needed answers.

And then this happened.

During a two-hour break between sessions, I thought that I would go for a bike ride, and during this ride I would think about who or what Kuan Yin was. It was as if I set out expecting Kuan Yin herself to speak up. For me, riding a bicycle often provides a sort of chemical shift—dopamine, endorphins, whatever—that can lift my mood and solve problems and questions, especially when I'm stuck while writing. Well, then, maybe it could also summon spirits! Wouldn't hurt to try!

So, I was cycling down a steep hill on a road through Fort Townsend State Park when I saw below me a woman on the right side of the road with a dog on a leash and an older man on the left side of the road walking unsteadily and drifting toward the middle of the road. I didn't want to frighten him, so I slowed and called out loudly, "Coming up!" hoping that he would move farther to the side of the road. Unfortunately my shout only startled him. He stumbled forward, lost his balance, and then fell face-first onto the road.

I stopped to make sure he was okay. His face was still on the road and his arms reached out helplessly, as if he didn't have control of them. He could not stand up on his own, so I put my bike down and tried to raise him. I assumed that he had had a stroke recently and was relearning how to walk. We needed to get him off the road as quickly as possible, but his wife was insisting that he get up on his own, saying, like some zealous personal trainer, "Come on! Get up! Use your arms!" That wasn't happening because he was like a bug on the end of a pin in a specimen box. I said to her, "Take his arm and let's get him up." We slowly got him to his knees and then to his feet.

The extraordinary thing was that when he stood and I looked into his face—glasses askew, dirty, humiliated, and in pain—I felt this profound sense of love for him and I said, "You're okay now, brother," and I embraced him. Stranger yet, I felt incredibly happy and grateful to him for this chance. It didn't feel like my actions were a consequence of being a "good person" acting out of ethical duty. It felt more like the man and I had stood together, in communion, "lost in a shaft of sunlight." It was a moment of complete connection without ego. Who was he? Who was I? Didn't matter. For his wife, though, this must have seemed a little strange. Help him up, sure, but call him brother and hug him? Not exactly the masculine American way, the "Aw shucks, ma'am, you're welcome" way.

Later, I was thinking about my experience and enjoying the memory of the feeling and it occurred to me that since I had been asking "Who is Kuan Yin?" for the last few days, specifically on this bike ride, perhaps she had answered me. She said, *This is who I am*, a little sly wink here perhaps, *and this is also who you are.*

Because it was not as if a literal god had appeared before us, like the Holy Ghost coming to Paul on the road to Damascus. As Tibetan Buddhism teaches, we were the deity, this suffering man and I. We had put on our "original face," if only for a moment. We had become who we really are, or as close to that as I have any hope of coming in what remains of what Dogen called my "timebeing."

Which is all pretty remarkable if you consider that nothing special had happened. Not really.

Nothing at all. That was its beauty.

Maybe this is just an example of how old men mutter to themselves about the "meaning of life." Or perhaps it is just the eternally trippy hippy in me still yammering metaphysics. Or maybe it's just "woo-woo" and I should be embarrassed. Beats me! Yes, and so, to conclude it, as his wife and I walked the poor man carefully across the road to their car, she said to him, "I'll drive."

—Curtis White, writer, San Lorenzo, CA

"IF WISDOM IS A SYSTEMIC FORM OF BELIEF," says my friend Mary Austin Speaker, "knowledge is a systemic form of understanding prone to errors in judgment, a getting lost. Belief needs nourishment, tending, roots, awareness. And adaptation, which can arrive as a form of kindness."[1] Nothing is small.

There's a moth dying in my hallway. Not dead. Dying, which is much worse because now I'm looking at something alive enough to need help, struggling enough that I would take notice, and one would imagine irrelevant enough that I wouldn't really care to be involved. So I ignored it the first time. Then I went back with a paper towel and picked it up, and the moth, in a final act of dramatic timing, chose that precise moment to die. I wonder if I killed it, or if it even knew it was dying. I left the moth on the paper towel and walked away. Then I went back, now for the second time, this time compelled to say a prayer. I couldn't save its life, but maybe I could save its soul? A dead bug. It was a saga that seemed out of all proportion . . . the reflex to care, even when, it would seem, there's nothing much to save.

—Rajeev Persaud, Hindu priest and chaplain, Mississauga, ON, Canada

The night I found Hank the temperature had fallen well below zero. It was three in the morning when I decided to walk over to the twenty-four-hour grocery store to get a snack and to roam the aisles, maybe wear out my anxiety so I could get some much-needed sleep.

Snow blanketed trees and the ground. I was barely through my building's parking lot when from the whiteout came a frantic chirping. Not even twenty feet in front of me, there was a bright-green flurry on top of the snow. It was a bird. *Strange,* I thought. *A brightly colored bird? In Colorado?* This was a budgie parakeet.

The bird was almost dead. His high-energy bursts became more sporadic and no matter how hard he tried, his wings wouldn't lift his tiny body off the ground. I had to save him. I tried to lift him but he was frozen to the ground. I had to peel his feet from the cement.

I rushed him up the stairs into my apartment and put him in the empty bathtub. This was one of those crazy things you want to tell somebody about. And it was Sara who I wanted to tell—but couldn't. She'd dumped me a week earlier, giving me a new breed of anxiety.

I bought the cheapest cage I could find and named the bird Hank. I put Hank in his new home and put his new home atop my bookcase.

I was so depressed about Sara that I rarely left my apartment. Days went by, Hank looking down on me wasting away on the couch.

One night Hank was using his head to lift the door to his cage open, then letting it slam shut. Over and over. Then he'd bob up and down, like he was taunting me.

"If you want out, get out then," I said. I flipped open the cage door and left it that way. I fell asleep. When I awoke several hours later, Hank was preening himself in the shivering blue of an after-hours infomercial. He stopped preening and fluffed his feathers. Right then, he appeared to me not as a bird but as a soft light. A beautiful warbling sound bubbled up from deep inside his soul. The same place a cat gets its purr or a Buddhist gets their OM. In that moment, I felt calmer than I had in a month. Then I noticed his feet. They were almost black. They'd been pink before.

Two days later Hank woke me whistling a happy tune. I went into the living room. Hank wasn't on his perch. I could make out the top of his head moving back and forth in the bottom of the cage. When I got up there to look, I saw that his feet were gone! They had broken off. Was it frostbite? How would he perch and land without his talons?

I customized his cage to accommodate his special needs. By day's end, he was getting around as if he'd never had legs to begin with. He walked around on his little nubs, going up and down the handicap ramp I made. His resilience blew me away. Thinking of what Hank went through made my troubles seem small. He was a survivor, and he survived for eight more years after this.

—Jason Hardung, writer, painter, and horticulturist, Cheyenne, WY

I LOVE THIS LAST STORY so much from my friend Jason Hardung, because in acting with such complete and total compassion for another, even in the midst of his own heartbreak, he is unknowingly holding up a mirror to himself. I know some really wonderful people in this world, and I don't think I've ever known anyone who is more of a (benevolent and resilient) survivor than Jason. I wish I could say more, but that is his story to tell, as he beautifully does in his memoir *Mammal*.[2] In her 1961 novel *Seduction of the Minotaur* (was there ever a better title?) Anaïs Nin writes, "We do not see things as they are, we see them as we are."[3] I am not sure I appreciate the difference, but I do appreciate why Albert Einstein said the most important decision we will ever make is whether we believe we live in a hostile or friendly universe.

In this next story, something at the heart of the life trajectory of the lawyer and animal advocate Carlos Contreras Lopez does a 180 because of the astonishing, incredible strength of his own mother in service of love and compassion amid almost unimaginable terror. To love this fiercely amid such suffering is remarkable. May each of us really absorb this—or at least be instructed by it.

My father taught me to distinguish between a guerrillero and a Colombian soldier by their boots. Rubber boots for the guerrillas to hide in the wet rainforest; leader combat boots for the soldiers to march on land. I wanted to be a guerrillero. They would come home every month and ask politely if we would like to be "vaccinated." Everybody would quickly agree and even beg them to take the money. In Spain, I would later learn, separatist terrorists called it the "revolutionary tax." The mafia called it the "protection wage" or *pizzo*. For us it was "vaccination." I was in awe of the way their reputation alone caused people to agree to anything they would suggest. I was unaware of how much cruelty such reputation costs, and the idea of having such power fascinated me. Then they kidnapped my dad.

The guerrilleros, once a group of idealist students fighting injustice, had turned into a ruthless gang that supplemented their income from drugs with routine abductions. Like them, my dad was a peasant who had moved to the city to attend a state university. While kidnapped, he had to move from camp to camp with the guerrillas, evading the army that pursued them to rescue him. They will be always moving, except when they set up camp and surround it with land mines, so that they could sit to eat some rice and yuca and sleep. If soldiers approached, the mines would explode, giving the guerrillas time to escape with their precious trophy (my dad).

In the woods, the casualties were unsuspecting animals who would explode into pieces. My father saw them explode. He also saw other former students explode. There is nothing more terrifying than seeing members of your own species die before your eyes. And he saw them lose their legs or their lives just meters away from him, until the guerrillas took him away to hide him better. Dad took refuge in writing and wrote to us daily letters we never received. Out of sheer malice, a guard snatched the notebook he was using and tore it apart. Even that small comfort was taken from him. We do not know what else they did to him. He had always told us that "boys don't cry." But when he was liberated, he was transformed and cried like a baby. Whenever he tried to explain to us what happened, he broke into tears and had to stop.

All we know was that he was not saved by the army, the police, a rival guerrilla, his male relatives, or some vigilantes. It was just Mum. She negotiated his release, speaking directly with the guerrillas. Her priority was to get him alive, and so she told the general of the Colombian army to mind his own business and stay away. The guerrillas had recruited peasant boys and girls, from age twelve onward, and handed them AK-47s to defend the camps, shooting before asking. They were dangerous children, but it would have been terrible to have to kill them to escape. My mum avoided the bloodshed [and Dad came home]. I no longer wanted to be guerrillero. It was better to be like her.

—*Carlos Contreras Lopez, lawyer and animal rights advocate, Bucaramanga, Colombia*

IF YOU ARE FORTUNATE ENOUGH to know Carlos, you know he means it and is living his life by this light. Might we join him and pause for a moment a quarter of the way through the twenty-first century and ask ourselves, *What kind of reality are we making here together—not only, of course, by our actions but also, and just as importantly, by way of the kinds of stories we tell and those we don't? Those we keep on the down-low or for whatever reasons, refuse to countenance? How is this shaping our world?*

As a person raised in a Catholic school system from age three to nine, I used to believe that if you told a lie, it was "bad" because there was an anthropomorphized God, kind of like Santa Claus, watching me and who would dole out a punishment. (The God we *experience,* writes Father Gregory Boyle, is uncaged and freed of [that] personified deity.[4]) Enough infractions and sometime, somehow, later, I would be in a place called hell. It would be fiery and hot.

At age six, observing the sacrament of penance, I gave my first confession to the head parishioner of our church and school: "I told my parents I had brushed my teeth, but I lied." How it tortured and shamed me to say this aloud to him. I was six. And, I thought, in big trouble. As would become customary, he gave me a certain number of Hail Marys and Our Fathers to recite back in my place in the pew. (Years later, in 2002, a Cuyahoga County grand jury would indict him on charges including sex abuse, rape, and compelling prostitution.)

Now I see lying differently. When a person lies—when I lie—I am weaving this lie into the seamless fabric of all that we are. What a thing to put there. What a way to use my will and the moments of my life. My lie becomes a part of a world, even the universe, that we are all creating together. And this, more than any white-bearded God or priest, or any fear of punishment or retribution, has changed the way I reflect upon my own behavior and wrongdoing—especially before I'm about to engage it. If, say, your cosmovision were one like Chuck Fowler's (his was the spiritual awakening prompted by consideration of the infinity symbol), and everything, everything, is connected in a net, and you tell a lie (even if you "never get caught" and "there is no hell"), how does that lie nevertheless change or contribute to the fabric of this universe at its furthest reaches? If a convicted felon—a liar and a cheater and a sex offender—is elected leader of the so-called free world, to what extent might you be personally responsible, even if you voted for "the other guy"? How much and of what did you contribute to the fabric of reality in which he becomes president? And would *that* be hell?

A more relational cosmovision reveals what truly formidable responsibility we have for this world. The ethical implications are profound. For the same reason, it is a pretty *empowering* worldview. If everything we do—every word, thought, action, motive, fear, sneeze, fart, howl, slice of toast, forest fire, lie, foggy dream—is part of a single fabric, is part of *this*, then there's some hope and agency therein. If you don't like the kinds of threads you're weaving into this fabric, if you don't like this fabric, change what you're working with. As earthlings, we know there are endless opportunities in a single hour alone to choose which threads we're going to weave the day with: Our good intentions? A pack of lies? Irritation? Follow-through? Attention? Distraction? Overwhelm? A six-pack? A piece of fruit? There are deep implications behind the apparent fact that we are not so separate from each other as our conditioning leads us to believe and that we are literally making this world together in real time. It does not exist behind us or around us. It does not exist *nearby*. It is not the background. It—this world—is as close to you and as intimate as your own guts. Your own headache. Enter fully into your lived experience. And know this: When you stand in front of your bedroom mirror, you are standing before the presence of the entire world. Nothing and no one is hidden.

Sounds like an impossible lot for any human being to hold in awareness or be awake to as they go about their day with its various contradictory demands, ambition, harsh realities, unceasing desire and/or keeping empire at bay. As Dale Jamieson says, "It is hard to live an ethical life,"[5] and this is increasingly true the broader our view of what is morally considerable (e.g., animals? trees? ecosystems? AI systems?). In fact, it seems to me that living an ethical life in awareness of a relational worldview and in the Anthropocene, facing what seem like and what may actually be insurmountable global problems . . . this may look a lot more like making spiritual vows than determining what reason alone—that is, what moral philosophy—deems to be the most sound ethical system.

A spiritual vow is about what we give our lives to, knowing we will fail. We take vows not because we can fulfill them but because we must. We don't reason our way into them so much as we surrender to them. And a vow has a life of its own; when you take a vow, you don't know where it's going to lead—as anyone who has taken marriage vows can attest, and as anyone who has divorced can attest. I myself have divorced; at the time, it was Egyoku Roshi (who also once divorced) who told me, "Not all decisions we make before we're thirty are going to hold our whole lives." Or before we're forty, I would add, or fifty. It was generous and freeing for her to say. And years later, she gave me a ceremony for *releasing* a vow, which many of us may feel the need to do.

Impossible spiritual vows are ancient and ubiquitous. The Buddhist chant to serve or save all sentient beings is one such vow. Hindus and Jains vow total abstention from harm—absolute nonviolence. Christians often recite the Prayer of Saint Francis: "Where there is hatred, let me sow love." And "Grant that I may not so much seek to be understood as to understand." Indeed, Jesus Christ asks that we love our enemies and turn the other cheek. In the Islamic tradition, vows of *zuhd* commit to living entirely detached from worldly possessions, status, and praise. Traditional Judaism contains 613 mitzvot; some contradict each other situationally, and some are impossible. There is a Lakota vow to be a "hollow bone": a pure vessel for spirit without any ego interference. As long as we are human, these vows are impossible to realize all the time or even much of the time. And yet we make them—some of us make them again and again, every morning and every evening, with sincerity and intention and clearness of heart . . . only to break the vow the moment we leave the temple, or the zendo, or the fire, or the hearth. We make these vows knowing we can never perfectly uphold them, which is precisely why we make them.

A vow is not a promise about the future, says Bernie Glassman, but a direction you walk in now.[6] These are words worth turning over a few million times.

I find compelling in this particular age the growing importance of spiritual work, spiritual resilience, and ethical imperatives that look like spiritual vows. There is a tension in examining, for example, our surrender to something like the next few centuries' worth of climate change effects (they can be mitigated now, but not stopped) with the kinds of lives we ought to live anyway (such as lives of temperance, collaboration, and minimizing harm). How do we live knowing we will fail, because to a serious and scientifically demonstrable extent, we have already failed?

In our unbalanced world, our news feeds—from memes to serious journalism—are overwhelmingly full of "solutions" and listicles of "ten ways to save" language; these are born of increasing and understandable anxiety, for there are many real and pressing sources of instability in our world. Some are driven by the natural cycles of geological epochs and others by the seasons of the year and the courses of an ordinary life. Among these sources of instability, for example, anthropogenic climate change has a special place, sparking a desperate search for what are called "climate solutions." But for there to be solutions there must be problems, and we need to be crystal clear about what the problem is that climate solutions are supposed to solve. Exactly what problem or problems are we trying to solve when we talk about saving the planet or protecting Earth? What cosmovision are we inhabiting when we make such statements? And how might efforts made from such grounds actually perpetuate the harm and destruction we are sincerely committed to ending?

The idea of "climate anxiety" (also called eco-grief or solastalgia) was triggered decades ago by the growing consciousness of air and water pollution. But the anxieties around climate change are deeper and more fundamental than what is suggested by the word *problem*. Scratch an environmental problem and you'll find profound questions about what we value and why, who we are and what we love, and how we grieve our various losses. In almost every case, you would find an entire cosmovision—a one-world cosmovision—trying to neatly circumscribe it all.

But there is no circle humans can draw that is vast enough to contain all that we are and how far we extend, first of all because there is no place to stand to draw it. There is no god's-eye view. We want that god's-eye view. And it is sometimes seriously useful theoretically to imagine we have it. But no matter how much we may wish to be elsewhere, no matter our capacity to imagine perhaps real "alternative" or "parallel" universes, in our human form, on Earth, on the moon, or on Mars, we are always looking out from an embedded position that starts where our feet meet the ground. So we may as well accept this and try to realize, as Frank Ostaseski says, that whatever ground we are on is holy.

On January 18, 2019, I boarded a plane from China back to Vietnam. I left China two days before school break actually started, and two weeks before COVID-19 spread around China and every international student was required to leave.

There was so much that I wished I had done differently. I wished that I had let myself loose more. I wished I was not so caught up in the academic pressure. I wished I had gone to more rooftop parties. I wished I had told my friends how much I treasured them. I wish

I could hold them in my arms and let them hold me in their arms. I wish I hadn't left China earlier. I wished I could see how our lives would unfold had the pandemic not happened.

We never thought the separation was permanent. Initially when we were informed that we would be doing online classes, I still nurtured the hope that we would always get back to that little island by the lake. It was only a matter of time. The whole time I was doing online school at home, I clung onto this hope as a lifeline. It was the imagined life, the parallel universe that kept me going in this universe. I imagined A.—my best friend—knocking on my door every Saturday morning, waking me up. I imagined going for breakfast at the university. I imagined coming into my room and finding notes from R. telling me that everything was going to be okay. I imagined us sitting in our usual classroom again reading Claudia Rankine's *Don't Let Me Be Lonely*.

Days turned into weeks, weeks turned into months, classes and late-night Zoom calls later, my naivete hope gave way to a feeling of numbness. I watched as the repetition of daily structure took hold of my life, desensitizing me into a walking zombie. And then, come August, when other high schools in the United World Colleges network established plans for their international students to come back to school, Changshu announced that China would not be opening its border. We, as international students, would be left with two options: transfer to another UWC or carry on with online learning. Those who could transfer transferred. Some who couldn't either stayed or dropped out. Even with those who chose to stay, most had had enough of online learning and chose to defer for another year. I watched as people transferred to other UWCs, my best friends dropping out and each going back to their respective country's educational system. I watched as my hopes of reunion shattered and the possibility of us getting back to school vanished into thin air. I felt like waking up in a sinking ship where everyone had evacuated except for me. I cried out for help, yet all I heard was my voice echoed back to myself.

I don't know what it was that kept me going through that year. I know part of it was because of R., my emotional counselor who called me every Monday morning—one of the things that I looked forward to every day. I know part of it was because of Z. I know part of it was reading into Tibetan Buddhism, practicing nonviolence, practicing groundlessness, touching that in-between state of uncertainty, practicing being with all the chaos that was happening.

I experienced déjà vu when, years later, I was finally leaving Vietnam again, this time for the United States. It took me a whole semester to come to terms with the fact that I was no longer in Vietnam, similar to how, when I came back from China, it took me weeks to register with the fact that I was really in Vietnam. Similarly, when I made plans with B. and Z. to meet over winter break freshman year in DC, I still did not quite register with the fact that I was actually going to meet them.

We did not have any specific plan in mind that night but to just roam the city. We went to an Ethiopian restaurant, biked around, and eventually ended up in Z.'s dorm room in his university. Z.'s current dorm had a strange resemblance to his room back in Changshu—still messy, still reeked with alcoholic smell, still very much himself. Later into the night, we started catching up. We talked about the old days in China, about Jimailong, about the rice daddy, about rooftopping. Z. talked about how the place changed after international students were gone. B. talked about his transition to a new environment, and I talked about my experience with online learning and the feat of not giving up. With music humming in the background, direct interactions, heartfelt conversation, I felt like we were back in China again.

We talked until 3 a.m. when Z. called his friends over and we went for a walk around the city. We went up to a monument. Although B. and Z. were drunk and mumbling, I found solace in their company. I left them to their friends, strolled to the staircase, and sat down. Staring into the distance, I burst into tears. I never thought I would survive the tumult and dread and loneliness of the pandemic; I never thought I'd be with my friends again, or even see them. And then—like a flash of lightning—that life was gone; totally gone!

At times, I still wonder what happened in that parallel universe, how it would have been if we had stayed those two years in China. When COVID happened, we went our separate ways. Z. was in China, B. transferred to Norway, I stayed in Vietnam. Now, by some stroke of luck, our paths had crossed again. There we were, not in China, not on that little island as we had promised, but here in DC. We all had changed, for better or for worse, but it was good to catch up on where we left off, perhaps as a conclusion to our ruptured journey. Even if we did not walk the same route and missed out on what happened in one another's lives in those two years, our path did cross again, in a different time and space.

But there I was here, instead, in this new moment of time, re-united, and in the United States, in Washington, DC. It was surreal. By which I mean it was totally real. Nothing imagined about it. There I was. There we were. Our feet on a shared piece of ground.

I wept.

During a fleeting conversation together, B. asked me how I defined home. In *False Papers: Essays on Memories and Exiles*, André Aciman writes that as an exile, home is neither a place, nor people. Rather, home is the traffic between different dimensions. It was the act of being in this dimension while remembering the other that was the act of homecoming.

Since then, the novelty, or the wonder, of that moment in DC somehow got replaced by a repetition of events: of classes to go to, of people to meet, of time to fill.

It is my sacred work to maintain awareness of that traffic between dimensions—it is happening all the time. I am always coming home. Now. And now. And now.

—Quân Nguyễn, doctoral student in chemistry, Hue, Vietnam

THE ABUNDANT REALITY AND NOVELTY of the presence now, and now, and now, overcame for Quân his imagined sense of a possible or parallel world. Henri Bergson writes, "For the possible is only the real with the addition of an act of mind which throws its image back into the past, once it has been enacted."[7] That is, the real is naked—and in response, you might weep, with gratitude or in sorrow as the case may be. The *possible* is an abstraction on top of this naked reality. This happens as a result of the kind of thinking action that my Zen teachers call "putting a head on top of" whatever actually is. The question is not where your feet could have been, where your feet might have been, or where your feet were or may someday be, but where are your feet right now? (Once, in response to asking my utterly wonderful eighth-grade algebra teacher, Candace Schultz, "When would I ever need to know this?" I received a very firm reply: "*Right now*.") Asking where our feet are right now is a question that could be of much service when considering our inability to address climate change. If we could agree on where we're standing in the present moment (dissenting voices from news media notwithstanding), we might be better able to agree upon rational (and perhaps compassionate) courses of action to address the situation. We might be better able to disentangle our anxiety about problems with solutions from conditions we must now learn to live with. And we might thereby have a better sense of how we *ought* to live.

Here's what I mean by distinguishing between problems and conditions. Mother Nature—as in many cultures we think of nature—provides the physical "building blocks" that structure the ways we live, manage our affairs, and organize our societies. Climate is an expression of these building blocks: It is a condition of our lives, much like the cultures and communities in which we are embedded, and the fact of our being embodied. But so often we confuse conditions with problems (maybe because we are frustrated by conditions we cannot engineer). Conditions are facts we must live with, while problems are open to solutions. The distinction between them is to some extent in the minds of the beholders. In the United States, for example, the authority of the electoral college helps to define what counts as constitutional presidential politics. Despite the anomalies it sometimes produces, it is generally regarded as a condition to live with rather than as a problem to be solved. We can imagine an American political system without an electoral college; what is difficult to imagine is how we might get there from here. And so we live with the electoral college as a condition of our collective political lives.

On the other hand, mass migration into the United States is often viewed as a problem, with "mass deportation" as the name of a solution. (Whether it is a real solution to a real problem is another matter.) A great deal of political rhetoric is aimed at framing matters either as conditions that we must live with or problems that can be solved with effective leadership. Recall the extent to which mortality itself is seen by some as a problem to be solved.

This framing struggle occurs daily and regularly even in each of our own minds. Is my propensity to choose toxic partners a condition I must live with and learn to work around, or is it a problem that I should grab by the scruff of the neck and banish from my life?

While conditions are not problems that we solve, they too are transient, for change is intrinsic to the conditions that govern life on Earth. What makes the climate change that is now underway different from the climate changes of the past is that it is anthropogenic. We are causing it, and we must learn to live with what we are bringing about. This brute fact is both a source and consequence of a confusing panoply of human emotions from guilt and regret to indifference and feelings of superiority over other living things.

Of course, it did not have to be this way; it is the outcome of a particular view of humans and their relationships with the nonhuman world. Nearly half a century ago, when the precautionary case for phasing out fossil fuels was consolidating, climate change was a problem that could have been solved or managed. But now the genie is out of the bottle and cannot be put back in, at least not on time scales we understand and care about. Electric cars, solar panels, energy-efficient appliances, and smart buildings—all of these are important, but they will not return the atmosphere to its preindustrial baseline.[8]

The fact is, we must learn to live with rising seas, more extreme weather, ecological disruption, and the ensuing human consequences including mass migration and intensifying conflict. Even geoengineering technologies that have the potential to radically alter Earth's energy balance are not solutions to the problem of climate change. They promise to remake the world and present us with different conditions for life on Earth, not return us to those of the past.

Psychological, physical, social, and yes, spiritual work and resilience are needed to survive and flourish in the future that we are creating.

Summoning the strength, expertise, wisdom, and motivation is difficult, for in fact we transform the planet for many good reasons: to feed a large and growing human population, to maintain health and comfort, to enable mobility beyond the dreams of most twentieth-century people and even many people today. However, we also design, build, and orchestrate systems that cater to relatively trivial desires: year-round seventy-degree indoor spaces, luxury foods (which in many cases require live animals to be shipped around the world under terrible conditions), golf courses and ski resorts in deserts, and other objects of our individual and collective fantasy. Most of the benefits from these ventures are harvested by the rich and powerful while the poor suffer most of the costs. Making matters worse, we know that these systems episodically fail in both predictable and unpredictable ways. As we look over the horizon to an increasingly unstable world, many of us are aware that this way of life cannot really continue. And we're right: It won't.

Our children may live in a world in which the seas have reclaimed Miami Beach and Miami itself has begun to reassemble as an island city. Likewise for Venice, Italy; Jakarta; Bangkok; Ho Chi Minh City; and many beaches of southern France. Tuvalu, Kiribati, the Maldives, the Marshall Islands. By then, several member states of the United Nations may have ceased to exist. What we have done and what is unfolding is so unfathomable that we often tune out the speed, scope, and scale of the changes that we are witnessing. Reason abandons us while anxiety remains.

Such enormous uncertainty raises spiritual, not just ethical, questions—questions that require us to allow meaning to emerge from our deeply embedded experiences and relationships with each other. Some will look to a political leader, oligarch, or technologists to save us from the consequences of our actions. Others simply pray: for justice, for the good life to continue, or for particular miracles—for a storm to change direction or a child to heal.

To be spiritually engaged and resilient means to hope for good outcomes and work with intelligence and compassion without expectation or attachment to success. Even on the small scale of everyday life, this kind of spiritual work is hard, and it can feel woefully inadequate to the enormity of the future we are facing. It can and may be impossible.

Climate change can worsen many of the challenges that require us to mobilize the resources of science, medicine, engineering, law, economics, politics, and the social sciences: migration, inequality, geopolitical instability, pandemic and other global health risks. But it also poses spiritual, philosophical, and therapeutic challenges: How can we survive and flourish in a world that we ourselves have created that threatens much of what we love and cherish?

This is the most profound question of our century and one that we have bequeathed to our children. Spiritual resilience is one of the many forms of mastery that climate change demands, and training ourselves and our children to bring this discipline to bear in the seasons and decades ahead is demanding work that we should embrace, for ourselves and for those who will come after us.

In the story below, almost from beginning to end, the Diné novelist Brendan Basham sees himself as part of the land. His body is the land, and the land is his body. "We are called to assist the Earth to heal her wounds and in the process heal our own," says the Kenyan activist Wangari Maathai.[9] But we cannot know, and must let go of, what shape we think healing will take. Basham both struggles with and accepts this; he becomes gently, playfully aware of his wish to fix what does not need human fixing—what is already resolving and healing without human engineering, but still with agency indeed (in Basham's words, the water thinks, and the woods give birth). I suppose accepting a darkness that resolves a disordered Earth and looks to us like death may indeed sound crazy, to some. I have read this a hundred times and am still finding new pockets and lines of feeling and wisdom in it.

I began thinking in swales in order to heal the land as I might heal myself. Until recently, I thought the word *swale* meant "barricade" or "dam," but a swale is really the indentation behind the hindrance—a hollow place, a depression. Somewhere deep in the high-desert woods surrounded by dormant volcanoes, I step outside into a mist ferrying petrichor and sweet pine, and I sit in the path of the sun's rise and watch as the light opens a lid where up pops orange and candy-corn bluffs grinning behind me. I listen to the birds, the ponderosa, piñon, and juniper trees centuries old, ancient enough that they're friends with the holy ones. These trees leak from their bark a savory-sweet butter and scotch brewed from their own blood. *How long did it take them to find the right chemistry?* I wonder.

These woods also birthed a white doe. I saw it the other day as I was counting the bathtub rings on the canyon walls, dreaming about when (or if) the water will return.

A swale is as powerful an image as it is a practice in understanding how water thinks. I invent a new verb: *swaling*—not to be confused with *swailing*, spelled with an *i*, which is a controlled burn, which also sounds awfully close to my attempt to orchestrate water.

Two German shepherds live on the land with me, and their hunting and wrestling can erode the fragile land quicker than it takes for flowers to rebound; grasses, brush, seeds, and trees to take root, further hindering the integrity of the earth. Without natural debris for seeds to cling to, more sand and crumbly stone will wash away. I want to postpone erosion caused by a combination of drought, erratic downpours, snowmelt and mud, the unrelenting winds. So, I set heavy volcanic rocks along sandy slopes with snap-happy sticks, broken brick, and chips of slate, constructing little barriers. I don't move stones from one spot to another just for aesthetic pleasure. I believe (perhaps naively) that I can "fix" the land to its natural state, return it to its untouched glory before ranchers disturbed its peace, before drought, before me and the dogs trample it further despite our delicate steps. I notice now that my tendency is to want to control things even though I lack control of anything, because the possession of control is illusory.

Inspired by a raven neighbor swooshing by on his way to work, I climb a tree and study the landscape from above, deciphering where the water wants to go, has gone. I shimmy back down and—further informed by the land's telltales—I drag logs, boulders, two railroad ties, and buckets of gravel from here to there, to build tiny dams, culverts. I stomp on twigs until they're mulch and sprinkle them evenly over hot bald spots. On hills and embankments, I arrange rocks into tiny levees to slow and guide the movement of water, pondering how water thinks.

The goal of my swales is not to control but to rehabilitate; to interact, converse, communicate, commune; to rebel rather than repel. Swales do not block or clog so much as they detour, digress. Staring at the bluffs, I wonder: *What darlings, and dangers, words can be.*

In the afternoons, the dogs tear up my swales and crush brittle habitat into dust with their playfulness. Makes me mad, initially. I've attempted to train them to stay on designated paths, but I've come to realize that their contagious joy is worth the futility of my swaling. Tomorrow I will take another shot at my terracing of hollows.

Perhaps I am overly fussy. If I see a bare space on the ground kicked free of bark or mulch by a clumsy step from a big dog or human, I feel compelled to equalize the coverage, to rake for uniformity, but nature doesn't grow wild if we interrupt its natural decay. In English, the Diné word *hozhó* means, approximately, "balance" or "harmony." Of course, there might be multitudes of definitions, but I suspect hozhó is something I'm overtly searching for on these short acres. Perhaps my obsessions contradict the concept of hozhó and my intentions are less Zen-like than I initially thought.

At dusk, I again watch the sun ignite the bathtub rings on canyon walls from a riparian age when the valley was an estuary. The evening is chillier than last night. The sudden drop in temperature forces me to change out of my shirt into flannel and fleece. A cold front is moving in quickly, I feel it, and I'm looking forward to watching snow flurries gloom and gobble up the lovely sun. If I fall asleep in rain or snow, my suprasternal notch will become a swale.

I am set to build the first woodstove fire of the season when I find a dead bluebird atop a bed of last season's embers, entombed in ash like a Pompeian. One of her wings frozen in time hid her face and beak as if she had been shy of Death. There is so much beauty in this somber violence that it feels like a contradiction, a paradox. Why do I feel guilt for being able to see the magic in the morose?

Some time passes before I decide to burn rather than bury *dólii.* I construct a tiny pyre in the woodstove with strips of juniper kindling and frayed bark, then with the strike of a match, the bird's feathers light up faster than crumpled newspaper. I sit in front of the fire and think about the amount of energy it took to grow dólii's beautiful, iridescent—and surprisingly combustible—feathers. *K'é*, a life force, my aunt might point out; maybe akin to qi. Now all of that life and time is converted into flame and pops and spark. The combustion of death can heat a home.

Through the window, I see the albino deer again. I wonder how she has survived in the wild, looking all electric like that. She won't last the winter unless we get a lot of snow, but I expect another dry winter.

The dark can be life-giving. Like swales redirecting water, death is merely a concave space behind the wall. Hozhó is Earth's Plender gap, the suprasternal notch. I want to find comfort in that hollow place behind the hindrance.

—Brendan Basham, writer, artist, and educator, Anchorage, AK

–11–
Gifts of Darkness

Did you suppose there would be no hand to take yours when you reached into the dark?

—CLARK STRAND, *Waking Up to the Dark*

I'd follow love into extinction.

—AYISHA SIDDIQA, "On Another Panel About Climate, They Ask Me to Sell the Future and All I've Got Is a Love Poem"

I've been working on *Gospel of the Lots of Lucy* for the last ten years. The book is being given to me, is offered to my hearing, from some being beyond me who I've understood to be the voice or spirit or intelligence of Lucy, who has been dead for over three million years. Lucy, the Australopithecus hominid ancestor of humanity, is the oldest ancestor of our species that we've yet found physical evidence of. We have her bones. We dug them up in Ethiopia.

We could hold her.

Gospel is a book of prophecies. Lucy reads the sunlight that falls on a specific rock as her method of divination. She's working in the ancient tradition of drawing lots, which includes the book's title inspiration, the *Gospel of the Lots of Mary*, a tiny fifth-century Coptic codex that would have been held in someone's palm, an answer from it exchanged for money.

One can arrive at Lucy's book of lots as a reader, as one would any book; or one can arrive at the book as a questioner and then, through bibliomancy, draw their lot (randomly select a page or a spot on a page) to receive their answer.

I hear Lucy differently now than I did when we first began writing the book together. Ten years ago, I . . . caught her words, now and then. I half-believed her voice was happening. I'd hear her, then jump in too quickly to finish her thought with my own thought. I'd improve upon her. I'd tweak or amplify or embolden or sharpen or cut something she was saying, using my own voice and aesthetics as a guide. I wasn't a dismissive person ten years ago, but I was new to our conversation.

When I first heard her, Lucy guided me through my father's death. A few years later, she was still with me when my mother died. She's been with me each time I sat down, almost daily, to write this book across a decade. She's steadfast, generous, patient, and also impatient. She feels as if she is growing and changing, as I am, during this collaboration.

When we first began writing together, she felt like aphorisms, or bits of wisdom, or psalms . . . and then I'd ungentle her words with my own embodied bent. I'd infuse her language with what I'd been encountering in my own life or in our shared political moment. I was still working with patterns and tones I'd used in previous books.

When we write together now, Lucy and I have deeper, slower, weirder, more surprising turns of tone than I do on my own. She uses more words than I do. She isn't shy about gently, and for a long time, holding court. She wouldn't balk at a thousand-page book. I'm briefer. Sharper. I roll my eyes more.

When I'm writing with her, I experience Lucy first as a tone. As a humming feeling. As a kind of space encountering another kind of space. I can both feel her and hear her. I know I've gotten it right if the thing . . . buzzes.

I spent at least a couple years entangling and disentangling my voice from hers. Now I feel we are writing in a hybrid voice that only exists in this collaboration.

I had to do a lot of work to become the person who could collaborate with her. A lot of walks. A lot of reading. A lot of yoga. A lot of meditating. A lot of becoming older. A lot of erasing. Among other practices, I started praying the Rosary again while writing this book. Lucy feels like Mary to me. Both Lucy and Mary feel like Thunder, Perfect Mind, to me. The space inside me feels more enormous because of this work together. I am filled with all kinds of buzzing spaces . . . which is similar to how she describes herself now.

Lucy has some specific things she's trying to tell us. She wants us to open our arms wide. She wants us to swallow mountains. She wants there to be a lot of mountains inside of us. She wants us to dig a well and to be a well. When I ask her, she will describe her life on Earth before she died. She loves to try to describe exactly what she looks like now, dead three million years—she's constructed of lakes that have no bottoms, and tubes. Everything about her thrums. Lucy thinks of herself as the Mary in Michelangelo's *Pietà,* lovingly holding humanity, dead in her arms.

Lucy is writing this because she wants to help us die. She wants to help each reader die, as we each inevitably move toward death, and she wants to help humanity die, as we inevitably move toward extinction. Lucy is an expert in both of these areas—she died, and her species went extinct.

—Sarah Vap, poet, Missoula, MT

YESTERDAY, when I talked with Sarah, she told me that Lucy is like all the mothers and grandmothers that ever were, in one thrum. Sarah is like that, too. After having read her manuscript in its entirety, I know that I, too, by way of Sarah's poems, have been invited into communication with the woman we named Lucy. Actually. And I have so many questions.

In his consideration of what is possible and what is real, Henri Bergson equates every scene of ordinary life with a work of art—while perhaps not of the same artistic worth as a Rembrandt or Velázquez, he says (I *do* disagree)—every "scene" of our lives is as every bit as unexpected as a masterful work of art.

> Philosophy stands to gain in finding some absolute in the moving world of phenomena. But we shall gain also in our feeling of greater joy and strength. Greater joy because the reality invented before our eyes will give each one of us, unceasingly, certain of the satisfactions which art at rare intervals procures for the privileged; it will reveal to us, beyond the fixity and monotony which our senses, hypnotized by our constant needs, at first perceived in it, ever-recurring novelty, the moving originality of things. But above all we shall have greater strength, for we shall feel we are participating, creators of ourselves, in the great work of creation which is the origin of all things and which goes on before our eyes. By getting hold of oneself, our faculty for acting will become intensified. Humbled heretofore in an attitude of obedience, slaves of certain vaguely-felt natural necessities, we shall once more stand erect, masters associated with a greater Master.[1]

It is this life and this world we are making, one moment at a time. I am uncertain about almost everything. I am not optimistic about Western civilization, and I don't believe in redemption. I am afraid for all of us. I am afraid for my children and I am afraid for myself. But one thing I am confident about is that creation and destruction—like joy and grief, and form and emptiness—arise together. Where there are annihilation and death, you can be sure somewhere, somehow, birth and life is happening. It may be so many fathoms deep or light years away, so far beyond even those mysteries we have begun to appreciate, that it may as well be that life itself has been extinguished.

There is a little Zen instruction on a teaching that attempts to explain why so much of this is so hard for humans to imagine.

> The ordinary person assumes that movement occurs only in space; they can't believe that coming and going is also an aspect of time. At best, they might accept the possibility of such a phenomenon. Human beings have invented radio and television—sounds and images move freely through space. But there is also a need for a kind of radio and television that can transmit comings and goings in time—such as from present to future, or future to past.[2]

According to the teaching this text is supposed to help us grasp, when it seems that life, for lack of a better word, is about to be extinguished, when it seems everything is about to perish, totally, there will still be a dragon projecting a great treasure in an undersea palace. This image is meant merely to lend our feeble human minds with a way of imagining this—whatever this is—continuing. Absolutely. Mercilessly. Endlessly. Perhaps this is where Lucy awaits us on a lake with no bottom. She will welcome us with arms wide and together we will swallow mountains.

As Ariana Reines says, "I don't know. I don't know."

One of this book's contributors, Aimee Bender, recently told me: "The mystery sustains." In recent years, I've felt more and more that indeed it is only the mystery that sustains. That the stories in this book strike many of us as strange or unbelievable is a symptom of a sickness that is cultural in origin and planetary in consequences.

These stories are messages from people who are not yet, not fully, or no longer held hostage by a single version of being human. Any one of the tales could be the sign of a need to restore relational attention to the world around us, the effect of having done so, or both—and dynamically so. It's not really enough to notice a synchronicity, or even to steer by or share it. It's to ask: What does this instance of mystery require of me? What obligation have I now incurred to the universe that has just revealed to me its intelligence? Finally, for now, I don't believe the purpose of sharing such stories is merely to validate each unusual human experience—though that's important—but also to begin to decenter the human entirely, to learn to listen to all that is nonhuman, requiring no less than the complete subordination of the human storyteller to the living world of which each of us is a part. The truly essential leap is not only to tell our stories—it is listening with a full body and listening long enough to hear what stories the *world* is telling *us*.

Afterword

When you grasp time, time itself cannot be grasped. When you do not grasp time, time itself is realized.[1]

Sometimes when I read Zen Master Dogen, I feel like I am listening to a quantum physicist trying to explain to me how atoms, electrons, and photons shape the universe.

All things are impermanent. When they appear, they are nothing other than impermanence.[2]

I might have a moment of understanding . . .

Each thing is whole, yet each thing is part of a whole. Each thing is neither this nor that, and yet it is this and that.[3]

. . . but in the end, I am stopped in my conventional tracks. Perhaps this is where I belong. Off trail, lost in a traceless wilderness.

Mountains are mountains, rivers are rivers. Yet when mountains are mountains, they are not mountains; when rivers are rivers, they are not rivers.[4]

In fact, in the spirit of this book *The Magpie Spoke to Me,* I do have a relevant "lost in the wilderness" story to share: In 1972, on a trip to Japan, I climbed Mount Fuji, and *the mountain swallowed me head to toe.*

Yes—head to toe. I am not speaking metaphorically. I was gone missing, without words or thoughts, into what seemed to be my true element. I was gone. Swallowed. And this very short story, this experience of being swallowed by a mountain, points to something else—something important that is the subject of this book: Sometimes, we have to go far away from the familiar and allow ourselves to experience something radical, at the very least unexpected, to shake loose narrow views constraining our life. To do so is to step toward, or into, the full human experience. And almost all the time, to go far away from the familiar, we have to come completely into where we are.

Once we find this landscape, as it were, where we can come alive by opening in this way, we begin to sense how difficult it is to say where one human ends and a mountain, say, begins. In such a moment, in such an encounter, we are being called to experience being human in the world not *as if* but *indeed* for the first moment ever. And we may find ourselves questioning what some "thing" like a mountain really is.

In Taoism, mountains are viewed as living, breathing, sacred beings. From the Taoist perspective, the energy that the mountain is made of is primordial energy that has existed since before the beginning of time. This energy is consolidated in the mountain, momentarily fixed, yet actually dynamic in form.

In Chinese and Japanese culture, mountains have long been associated with meditation and purification, and are gateways to the god realm, and were sources of knowledge, discipline, and power.

I am grateful to have entrusted myself to Mount Fuji. *Entrust* is the right word. The degree to which we entrust ourselves to a mountain, or a river, or a neighborhood, or a roomful of people or to all of it, together—this is the degree to which we experience true belonging and—dare a Zen teacher say it?—love. There is abundance, fullness, and completeness in the experience of belonging in such a way. We might ask ourselves what it means to belong in such a way. Dogen, for one, meant that it means to love. People may have an idea about Zen that we don't get into this whole "love" thing. We wear black. We sit in silence. We have no attachments, right? But Dogen did not turn away from love in his texts. He did not turn away from these deep experiences of mutuality, of interdependence, of being swallowed up by a mountain, even as the mountain itself disappears.

Many of us have had at least some flash or glimpse of the love and belonging that make themselves felt so sharply, and so obviously, when even in the midst of great suffering or despair, we are for just a moment fully embodied and decentered. When our conditioned views about existence don't seem to match up with a physical experience we've had.

Part of what Bonnie is pointing to in this book is that our work lies in whether and how we open, then respond to such experiences; whether we trust our bodies and senses when we experience them; and how to then offer them, in service, sometimes as stories, to others.

"Let me tell you about the time I was swallowed by mountain," I might say to her. "I really was. Something happened to me up there on Mount Fuji."

"Tell me about it," she might then say, "and I'll tell you about the magpie, who told me the most beautiful thing."

Then we'd pour our tea, and we'd talk, and listen, and listen, and talk.

As the Taoist saying goes,

They passed eons living alone in the mountains and forests;
Only then did they unite with the Way,
And use the mountains and rivers for words,
And raise the wind and the rain for a tongue.

As with the wind and rain, so with a magpie. Can you hear them? Step fully into and trust your lived experience. Entrust yourself to your own attention, to your breath. Where are your feet, right now? What is the light like around you? What are you hearing? It takes deep and abiding attention to be fully human.

Why hold back? Yes, we can turn away from our lived experiences and the ways they challenge our relationship to each other and the world. We have that choice, and we have devised ingenious and myriad ways to turn away from them. But we can also turn toward our experiences.

Why not? It is not a rhetorical but a real question to ponder, and one that this book engages quite seriously. We have so very many reasons why *not* to trust and turn toward our lived experience, don't we? And, thank you very much, we already know quite well—do we not?—where one human ends and another begins. Can we not point clearly to where our own hand stops and the woods or the desert or the parking lot or the war zone begins?

As *The Magpie Spoke to Me* suggests and explores, we are creating a world, here, one moment at a time, by way of response to the experiences we have and the stories we tell (or not) about them. Pay attention to your lived experience. And listen—with all of your ears and eyes and hands—to everyone and everything around you.

As my old friend Dr. Carl Bielefeldt writes,

> Dogen says that although wise men and sages always enter the mountains, you can never meet one there; not even a trace of them remains. They seem to merge with the place, making the mountains, as Dogen says, "their own bodies and minds." If the mountains and waters can themselves become wise men and sages, I guess we shouldn't be surprised when the sages become mountains.[5]

Or even when the grass and trees do, Dogen reminds us. Even the walls.

—JOAN HALIFAX
Upaya Zen Centers
Santa Fe, New Mexico, 2025

Acknowledgments

WITH REVERENCE, GREAT RESPECT, AND DEEP AFFECTION, I thank each of you who has contributed to this book by sharing a personal experience. I have accepted each offering as sacred, because it is. May each of your stories be received with gratitude and passed on in the spirit of expanding our circle of kinship, and acting, when we do, in love. May our shared stories and voices be met with recognition, relief, and many, many more such tales. May they connect us in acceptance, serious thinking, and formidable responsibility. And may the mystery itself sustain. I thank particularly my editor, Peter Schumacher, and Jane Hirshfield and Joan Halifax.

Notes

Introduction

1. Alice Walker, "Am I Blue?" in *Living by the Word: Essays* (Harcourt Brace Jovanovich, 1989), 7.

1. Ghosts?

1. Walt Whitman, *Leaves of Grass*, ed. Malcolm Cowley (Penguin Classics, 1986), 26.
2. Immanuel Kant, *Critique of Judgment*, trans. Werner S. Pluhar (Hackett Publishing, 1987), 175.
3. Karl Popper, *Conjectures and Refutations: The Growth of Scientific Knowledge* (Routledge & Kegan Paul, 1963), 29.
4. D. H. Lawrence, *The Letters of D. H. Lawrence*, ed. James T. Boulton, vol. 1 (Cambridge University Press, 1979), 503.

3. Cosmovisions

1. See, for example, Clifford Geertz, *The Interpretation of Cultures* (Basic Books, 1973), 3–30; Claude Lévi-Strauss, *Structural Anthropology*, trans. Claire Jacobson and Brooke Grundfest Schoepf (Basic Books, 1963), 206–31; Bronislaw Malinowski, *Myth in Primitive Psychology* (Kegan Paul, 1926), 79–101; Jerome Bruner, *Acts of Meaning* (Harvard University Press, 1990), 33–54; Mircea Eliade, *Myth and Reality*, trans. Willard R. Trask (Harper & Row, 1963), 5–18.
2. Ashish Kothari, Ariel Salleh, Arturo Escobar, Federico Demaria, and Alberto Acosta, "Introduction: Finding Pluriversal Paths," in *Pluriverse: A Post-Development Dictionary*, ed. Ashish Kothari, Ariel Salleh, Arturo Escobar, Federico Demaria, and Alberto Acosta (Tulika Books, 2019), 1–18.
3. Annie Dillard, *Pilgrim at Tinker Creek* (Harper's Magazine Press, 1974), 35.
4. "Identity of Relative and Absolute," *Zen Mountain Monastery*, accessed January 6, 2026, https://zmm.org/teachings-and-training/identity-of-relative-and-absolute/.
5. Henri Bergson, *The Creative Mind: An Introduction to Metaphysics*, trans. Mabelle L. Andison (Philosophical Library, 1946).

6. Joan Halifax, *Being with Dying: Cultivating Compassion and Fearlessness in the Presence of Death* (Shambhala Publications, 2024), 123.
7. Edgar Morin and Anne Brigitte Kern, *Homeland Earth: A Manifesto for the New Millennium*, trans. Sean M. Kelly and Roger LaPointe (Hampton Press, 1999), 66.
8. Ralph Waldo Emerson, "The Over-Soul," in *Essays and English Traits by Ralph Waldo Emerson*, The Harvard Classics, ed. Charles W. Eliot (P. F. Collier & Son, 1909), 140.
9. John Law, "What's Wrong with a One-World World?" *Distinktion: Scandinavian Journal of Social Theory* 16, no. 1 (2015): 126–39.
10. Kothari et al., "Introduction: Finding Pluriversal Paths," 1–18.
11. Kimberly Hutchings, "Decolonizing Global Ethics: Thinking with the Pluriverse," *Ethics & International Affairs* 33, no. 2 (Summer 2019): 115–25.
12. Deepak Malghan, "Efficiency," in *Pluriverse: A Post-Development Dictionary*, ed. Ashish Kothari, Ariel Salleh, Arturo Escobar, Federico Demaria, and Alberto Acosta (Tulika Books, 2019), 50–52.
13. Amaya Querejazu, "Encountering the Pluriverse: Looking for Alternatives in Other Worlds," *Revista Brasileira de Política Internacional* 59, no. 2 (2016): e007.
14. Mario Blaser, "Ontology and Indigeneity: On the Political Ontology of Heterogenous Assemblages," *Cultural Geographies* 21, no. 1 (2012): 49–58.
15. Kothari et al., "Introduction: Finding Pluriversal Paths," 1–18.
16. Kothari et al., "Introduction: Finding Pluriversal Paths," 1–18; Jerome S. Bernstein, *Living in the Borderland: The Evolution of Consciousness and the Challenge of Healing Trauma* (Routledge, 2005).
17. Kothari et al., "Introduction: Finding Pluriversal Paths," 1–18.
18. Hutchings, "Decolonizing Global Ethics," 115–25.
19. *Ocampo-Raeder's note: Molcajetes* are a traditional Mexican mortar and pestle made from a wide variety of volcanic materials found throughout the central regions of the country.
20. *Ocampo-Raeder's note:* Pulque is a kind of mead made by fermenting the sweet sap of a particular variety of agave. It is not distilled as in the case of mezcales such as tequila.
21. Querejazu, "Encountering the Pluriverse," e007; Law, "What's Wrong with a One-World World?" 126–39; Bonnie Nadzam and Dale Jamieson, *Love in the Anthropocene* (OR Books, 2015).
22. Donna J. Haraway, "Situated Knowledges: The Science Question in Feminism and the Privilege of Partial Perspective," *Feminist Studies* 14, no. 3 (1988): 575–99; Hilary Putnam, *The Collapse of the Fact/Value Dichotomy and Other Essays* (Harvard University Press, 2002); Law, "What's Wrong with a One-World World?" 126–39; Arturo Escobar, *Designs for the Pluriverse: Radical Interdependence, Autonomy, and the Making of Worlds* (Duke University Press, 2018); Michel Foucault, *The Order of Things: An Archaeology of the Human Sciences* (Vintage Books, 1994); Immanuel Kant, *Critique of Pure Reason*, trans. Paul Guyer and Allen W. Wood (Cambridge University Press, 1998).
23. Henry George Liddell, Robert Scott, and Henry Stuart Jones, *A Greek–English Lexicon*, rev. ed. (Clarendon Press, 1996).

24. Martin Heidegger, "Science and Reflection," in *The Question Concerning Technology and Other Essays*, trans. William Lovitt (Harper & Row, 1977), 155–82; Andrea Wilson Nightingale, *Spectacles of Truth in Classical Greek Philosophy: Theōria in Its Cultural Context* (Cambridge University Press, 2004).
25. Kothari et al., "Introduction: Finding Pluriversal Paths," 1–18.
26. Philip McMichael, "Hidden Ideology," in *Pluriverse: A Post-Development Dictionary*, ed. Ashish Kothari, Ariel Salleh, Arturo Escobar, Federico Demaria, and Alberto Acosta (Tulika Books, 2019), 12–15.

4. Being Human

1. Neil Theise, *Notes on Complexity: A Scientific Theory of Connection, Consciousness, and Being* (Spiegel & Grau, 2023), 48.
2. Gregory Boyle, *Cherished Belonging: The Healing Power of Love in a Divided World* (Avid Reader Press, 2024), 12.
3. David Bohm, *Wholeness and the Implicate Order* (Routledge & Kegan Paul, 1980), 2.
4. Thomas Merton, *The Hidden Ground of Love: The Letters of Thomas Merton on Religious Experience and Social Concerns*, ed. William Henry Shannon (Farrar, Straus & Giroux, 1985), x.
5. Octavia E. Butler, *Parable of the Sower* (Four Walls Eight Windows, 1993), 3.

5. Storytelling, and Storytelling

1. Ian Watt, *The Rise of the Novel: Studies in Defoe, Richardson, and Fielding* (University of California Press, 1957); Michael McKeon, *The Origins of the English Novel, 1600–1740* (Johns Hopkins University Press, 1987).
2. Laurence Sterne, *The Life and Opinions of Tristram Shandy, Gentleman*, ed. Melvyn New and Joan New (Penguin Books, 2003); Samuel Richardson, *Clarissa, or The History of a Young Lady*, ed. Angus Ross (Penguin Books, 1986).
3. Jane Austen, *Emma*, ed. Juliette Wells (Penguin Books, 2015); Nancy Armstrong, *How Novels Think: The Limits of Individualism from 1719–1900* (Columbia University Press, 2006); Ian Watt, *The Rise of the Novel: Studies in Defoe, Richardson, and Fielding* (University of California Press, 2001).
4. Ian McEwan, *Atonement* (Jonathan Cape, 2001).
5. As Salesses has argued directly, "show, don't tell" itself is one of the inherited workshop axioms often presented as universal craft when it is better understood as a culturally specific norm. Matthew Salesses, *Craft in the Real World: Rethinking Fiction Writing and Workshopping* (Catapult, 2021).
6. Percy Lubbock, *The Craft of Fiction* (Charles Scribner's Sons, 1921); Mark McGurl, *The Program Era: Postwar Fiction and the Rise of Creative Writing* (Harvard University Press, 2009); "Show or Tell: Should Creative Writing Be Taught?" Louis Menand, *The New Yorker*, June 8, 2009, https://www.newyorker.com/magazine/2009/06/08/show-or-tell.
7. Gérard Genette, *Narrative Discourse: An Essay in Method*, trans. Jane E. Lewin (Cornell University Press, 1980). Genette's narratology is useful precisely because it treats scene and summary as alternating components of narrative discourse rather than as a hierarchy in which scene is good writing and summary is failure.

8. Barthes's "reality effect" remains decisive here because it shows that realist detail does not transparently deliver the real so much as produce the sign of the real. Roland Barthes, "The Reality Effect," in *The Rustle of Language*, trans. Richard Howard (University of California Press, 1989). Saint-Amour sharpens the point by showing how such effects can consecrate the gap between what exists and what has meaning, which is very close to the separation I am trying to describe. Paul K. Saint-Amour, "Alternate-Reality Effects," *PMLA* 134, no. 5 (2019): 1136–42.
9. "Alternate-Reality Effects"; Menand, "Show or Tell"; McGurl, *The Program Era*.
10. Gardner, *The Art of Fiction*; Menand, "Show or Tell"; McGurl, *The Program Era*.
11. Amitav Ghosh, *The Great Derangement: Climate Change and the Unthinkable* (University of Chicago Press, 2016); Nancy Armstrong, *How Novels Think*.
12. Perdita Finn, "Conversations with the Dead," online lecture series, Take Back the Magic, September–November 2022, https://takebackthemagic.com/.

6. No Analysis

1. John Keats, "Selections from Keats's Letters," Poetry Foundation, published October 12, 2009, https://www.poetryfoundation.org/articles/69384/selections-from-keatss-letters.
2. Dogen, *Treasury of the True Dharma Eye: Zen Master Dōgen's Shōbōgenzō*, trans. Kazuaki Tanahashi (Shambhala, 2010), 30.
3. Nisargadatta Maharaj, *I Am That: Talks with Sri Nisargadatta Maharaj*, trans. Maurice Frydman (Acorn Press, 1973), 153.
4. Dongshan Liangjie, "Song of the Jewel Mirror Samadhi," quoted in Taigen Dan Leighton, *Just This Is It: Dongshan and the Practice of Suchness* (Shambhala Publications, 2015), 169.
5. Francis Bacon, "*Aphorism XLVI*" in *Novum Organum*, Kimball Essays, University of Oregon, accessed March 10, 2026, https://pages.uoregon.edu/kimball/Bacon.htm.

7. Ordinary Relationship

1. Pádraig Ó Tuama, *Being Here: Prayers for Curiosity, Justice, and Love* (Convergent Books, 2018).
2. Joan Halifax, *Being with Dying: Cultivating Compassion and Fearlessness in the Presence of Death* (Shambhala Publications, 2024), 19.
3. Robert Lanza and Bob Berman, *Biocentrism: How Life and Consciousness Are the Keys to Understanding the True Nature of the Universe* (BenBella Books, 2009), 140.
4. Jerome S. Bernstein, *Living in the Borderland: The Evolution of Consciousness and the Challenge of Healing Trauma* (Routledge, 2005).
5. Ralph Waldo Emerson, "Experience," in *Essays: Second Series, new and rev. ed.* (The Riverside Press, 1883), 66.

8. Death and Dying

1. Zhuangzi, "The Seal of Virtue," in The Writings of Chuang Tzu, trans. James Legge (1891), https://ctext.org/zhuangzi/seal-of-virtue-complete.

2. Michel de Montaigne, *The Complete Essays,* trans. M. A. Screech (Penguin Classics, 1991), chapter 20.
3. Joanne Cacciatore, *Bearing the Unbearable: Love, Loss, and the Heartbreaking Path of Grief* (Wisdom Publications, 2017), 2.
4. Dalai Lama and Howard C. Cutler, *The Art of Happiness: A Handbook for Living* (Riverhead Books, 1998). Emphasis my own.
5. Francis Weller, *The Wild Edge of Sorrow: Rituals of Renewal and the Sacred Work of Grief* (North Atlantic Books, 2015), 25.
6. Ezra Klein, host, *The Ezra Klein Show,* podcast, "What It Means to Be Kind in a Cruel World," February 19, 2021.
7. Michael Mechanic, *Jackpot: How the Super-Rich Really Live—and How Their Wealth Harms Us All* (Simon & Schuster, 2021); Douglas Rushkoff, "Survival of the Richest: The Wealthy Are Plotting to Leave Us Behind," *The Guardian,* July 23, 2018, https://www.theguardian.com/technology/2018/jul/23/tech-industry-wealth-futurism-transhumanism-singularity.
8. Edgar Morin and Anne Brigitte Kern, *Homeland Earth: A Manifesto for the New Millennium,* trans. Sean M. Kelly and Roger LaPointe (Hampton Press, 1999), 133.
9. Annie Dillard, *Teaching a Stone to Talk: Expeditions and Encounters* (Harper & Row, 1982).
10. Perdita Finn, "Conversations with the Dead," online lecture series, Take Back the Magic, September–November 2022, https://takebackthemagic.com/.
11. Morin and Kern, *Homeland Earth,* 45.
12. Morin and Kern, *Homeland Earth,* 135.
13. Morin and Kern, *Homeland Earth,* 45.
14. Morin and Kern, *Homeland Earth,* 45.
15. Finn, "Conversations with the Dead."
16. Morin and Kern, *Homeland Earth.*

9. Grief

1. Gregory Boyle, *Tattoos on the Heart: The Power of Boundless Compassion* (Free Press, 2010).
2. John W. James and Russell P. Friedman, *When Children Grieve: For Adults to Help Children Deal with Death, Divorce, Pet Loss, Moving, and Other Losses* (HarperCollins, 2001).
3. Ann Linder, Bonnie Nadzam, Dale Jamieson, Kristen Stilt, and Valerie McCarthy, *Animal Markets and Zoonotic Disease Risk: A Global Synthesis of a 15-Country Study,* Brooks McCormick Jr. Animal Law & Policy Program, Harvard Law School and Center for Environmental and Animal Protection, New York University, 2024, https://animal.law.harvard.edu/wp-content/uploads/Animal-Markets-and-Zoonotic-Disease-Risk-high-resolution.pdf.
4. Sophie Kevany, "More Than 20 Million Farm Animals Die on Way to Abattoir in US Every Year," *The Guardian,* June 15, 2022, https://www.theguardian.com/environment/2022/jun/15/more-than-20-million-farm-animals-die-on-way-to-abattoir-in-us-every-year.
5. Linder et al., *Animal Markets and Zoonotic Disease Risk.*

6. Linder et al., *Animal Markets and Zoonotic Disease Risk.*
7. Dale Jamieson, *Ethics and the Environment: An Introduction*, 2nd ed. (Cambridge University Press, 2024), 234.
8. Joanne Cacciatore, *Bearing the Unbearable: Love, Loss, and the Heartbreaking Path of Grief* (Wisdom Publications, 2017), 3–4.

10. Responsibility

1. Mary Austin Speaker, email message to author, February 12, 2026.
2. Jason Hardung, *Mammal* (Thiessen Press, 2026).
3. Anaïs Nin, *Seduction of the Minotaur* (Swallow Press, 1961), 124. Here, Nin is referencing the Talmud, adding spiritual dimension to her claim.
4. Gregory Boyle, *Tattoos on the Heart: The Power of Boundless Compassion* (Free Press, 2010).
5. Dale Jamieson, *Ethics and the Environment: An Introduction* (Cambridge University Press, 2008), 150.
6. Bernie Glassman, *Bearing Witness: A Zen Master's Lessons in Making Peace* (Bell Tower, 1998).
7. Henri Bergson, *The Creative Mind: An Introduction to Metaphysics*, trans. Mabelle L. Andison (Philosophical Library, 1946), 112–13.
8. Intergovernmental Panel on Climate Change (IPCC), *Climate Change 2022: Mitigation of Climate Change* (Cambridge University Press, 2022), https://www.ipcc.ch/report/ar6/wg3/; Intergovernmental Panel on Climate Change (IPCC), *Global Warming of 1.5°C* (IPCC, 2018), https://www.ipcc.ch/sr15/; Foundation for Climate Restoration, *Climate Restoration: Returning the Planet to a Safe and Healthy State* (Foundation for Climate Restoration, 2022), https://foundationforclimaterestoration.org/wp-content/uploads/2022/02/whitepaper.pdf.
9. Wangari Maathai, "Nobel Prize Lecture" (speech, Oslo, Norway, December 10, 2004) The Nobel Prize, https://www.nobelprize.org/prizes/peace/2004/maathai/lecture/.

11. Gifts of Darkness

1. Henri Bergson, *The Creative Mind: An Introduction to Metaphysics*, trans. Mabelle L. Andison (Philosophical Library, 2007), 86.
2. This is from a restricted text belonging to my lineage.

Afterword by Joan Halifax

1. Ehei Dogen, *Treasury of the True Dharma Eye: Dōgen's Shōbōgenzō*, trans. Sōtō Zen Text Project (University of Hawai'i Press, 2025).
2. Dogen, *Treasury of the True Dharma Eye.*
3. Dogen, *Treasury of the True Dharma Eye.*
4. Dogen, *Treasury of the True Dharma Eye.*
5. Dogen, *Treasury of the True Dharma Eye.*

About the Author

BONNIE NADZAM is an American writer and Zen Buddhist priest and chaplain. Her poetry, essays, and fiction have appeared in *Harper's*, *Orion Magazine*, *The Iowa Review*, *Kenyon Review*, and many other journals and magazines. Her first novel, *Lamb*, was the recipient of The Center for Fiction's Flaherty-Dunnan First Novel Prize, translated into several languages, and made into an award-winning independent film. Her second novel, *Lions*, was a finalist for the PEN USA Literary Award in Fiction. She is also coauthor of *Love in the Anthropocene* with environmental ethicist Dale Jamieson. She is currently associate director of Ethics, Culture, and Religion with the Animal Law and Policy Program at Harvard University.